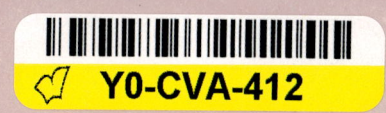

Presented to

Keri Plichta

By

Marge Alex

On the Occasion of

De Colors

Date

Aug 21, 2009

I Love You

365 ONE-MINUTE MEDITATIONS

DAILY WISDOM FOR WOMEN

365 ONE-MINUTE MEDITATIONS

DAILY WISDOM FOR WOMEN

FROM THE BESTSELLING DEVOTIONAL

Carol L. Fitzpatrick

© 2009 by Barbour Publishing, Inc.

Compiled by Rachel Quillin.

ISBN 978-1-60260-371-4

All rights reserved. No part of this publication may be reproduced or transmitted for commercial purposes, except for brief quotations in printed reviews, without written permission of the publisher.

Churches and other noncommercial interests may reproduce portions of this book without the express written permission of Barbour Publishing, provided that the text does not exceed 500 words and that the text is not material quoted from another publisher. When reproducing text from this book, include the following credit line: "From (name of book), published by Barbour Publishing, Inc. Used by permission."

Scripture quotations, unless otherwise noted, are taken from the New American Standard Bible, © 1960, 1962, 1963, 1968, 1971, 1972, 1973, 1975, 1977, 1995 by The Lockman Foundation. Used by permission.

Scripture quotations marked NIV are taken from the HOLY BIBLE, NEW INTERNATIONAL VERSION®. NIV®. Copyright © 1973, 1978, 1984 by International Bible Society. Used by permission of Zondervan. All rights reserved.

Scripture quotations marked NKJV are taken from the New King James Version®. Copyright © 1982 by Thomas Nelson, Inc. Used by permission. All rights reserved.

Scripture quotations marked KJV are taken from the King James Version of the Bible.

Cover image © Dave Michaels/zefa/Corbis

Published by Barbour Publishing, Inc., P.O. Box 719, Uhrichsville, Ohio 44683, www.barbourbooks.com

Our mission is to publish and distribute inspirational products offering exceptional value and biblical encouragement to the masses.

Printed in India.

A MINUTE A DAY CAN CHANGE YOUR LIFE.

We're all busy and pressed for time. But somewhere in our daily schedule, there must be at least sixty free seconds. Look for that open minute and fill it with this book. *365 One-Minute Meditations: Daily Wisdom for Women* provides a quick but powerful reading for every day of the year, promising real spiritual impact. Each day's entry features a carefully selected verse from God's Word, along with a condensed reading from *Daily Wisdom for Women*, the best-selling daily devotional by Carol L. Fitzpatrick.

First published in 1997, *Daily Wisdom for Women* has continued to offer practical, biblical insight for today's woman.

If you're seeking a spiritual lift, try *365 One-Minute Meditations: Daily Wisdom for Women*. You'll only need a moment per day—but the benefits could be life-changing.

Daily Wisdom for Women

CREATED BY GOD

*So God created man in his own image,
in the image of God he created him; male and female he created them.*

GENESIS 1:27 NIV

You are a woman; you were created in God's own image. God made you so that He might have an ongoing relationship with you. You need Him and He's promised to always be there for you. Isn't that the kind of life-companion you've searched for?

One-Minute Meditations

In the Garden

When the woman saw that the tree was good for food...
she took from its fruit and ate; and she gave also to her husband.

Genesis 3:6

Eve stood beside the "tree of the knowledge of good and evil" (Genesis 2:17) and chose to ignore the truth of God's Word. Adam and Eve were forced out of this physical garden. Years later, Jesus returned, and on the cross the sacrifice of His life provided forgiveness, allowing access to God's presence.

Daily Wisdom for Women

Seeking Wisdom

A wise man will hear and increase in learning.

Proverbs 1:5

When asked by God what he wished, Solomon answered, "Wisdom." If you'd been afforded this opportunity in your early twenties, what would your response have been? At that age wisdom probably wasn't high on your priority list. Instead of asking God for direction, you likely would have turned to your peers.

But God is with you. He's promised to give you the power to withstand moral crises.

One-Minute Meditations

The Rainbow

*I have set my rainbow in the clouds,
and it will be the sign of the covenant between me and the earth.*

GENESIS 9:13 NIV

Every day God freely displays His blessings. Are we too busy or disinterested to appreciate their wonder? Even if we've forgotten He's there, reminders are all around for He is the God of covenants. In a world where promises (or covenants) are disregarded routinely, I need God's kind of stability.

Daily Wisdom for Women

JANUARY 5

FISHERS OF MEN

"Come, follow me. . .I will make you fishers of men."

MATTHEW 4:19 NIV

Why did Christ want these fishermen? [They] were men of action who knew how to get a job done. Their tenacity would be an asset to Christ's ministry.

Jesus came not only to save but to teach men and women how to have servants' hearts. The substance of ministry is service. When the apostles agreed to follow Christ, they accepted the call on His terms.

One-Minute Meditations

Our Prayer Requests

*In the morning I lay my requests
before you and wait in expectation.*

PSALM 5:3 NIV

On Sunday evenings I would ask my husband and children for anything they'd like me to pray about. Often in the morning I'd find notes on my prayer chair. I wish I'd saved some of those. I do have memories of the celebrating we did when one of those prayers was answered.

Are you laying your requests before the Lord?

Daily Wisdom for Women

A Child of Promise

"Then I will bless her, and she shall be a mother of nations; kings of peoples will come from her."

Genesis 17:16

Long past childbearing age, Sarah had given up hope of ever cradling a babe of her own. And then when her husband, Abraham, was ninety-nine years old, the Lord made a covenant with him concerning his future heir. How gracious He is, even when we see no reason to hope.

One-Minute Meditations

VOCALIZING A PRAYER

*"And when you are praying,
do not use meaningless repetition."*

MATTHEW 6:7

As we come before the Lord, we first need to honor and praise Him. Because we're human, we need to confess and repent of our daily sins. Following this, we should be in a mode of thanksgiving. Finally, our prayer requests should be upheld. Your prayers certainly don't have to be elaborate. God knows your heart. He wants to hear from you.

Daily Wisdom for Women

Turn Your Ear to Wisdom

*For the LORD gives wisdom;
from His mouth come knowledge and understanding.*

PROVERBS 2:6

God's Word says wisdom is truly a gift since it comes from the mouth of God, from the very words He speaks. And all God's Words have been written down for us, through the inspiration of the Holy Spirit. Know that if you hold fast to the precepts contained in the Bible, you will walk on the straight and narrow road.

One-Minute Meditations

Sodom and Gomorrah

"The outcry of Sodom and Gomorrah is indeed great, and their sin is exceedingly grave."

Genesis 18:20

This grave sin of which God speaks is homosexuality. While the world may refer to this behavior as a "lifestyle," God says that it is vile. When His judgment did fall on the wicked cities of Sodom and Gomorrah, it was swift and terrible. When God says flee, don't try to hold on to sin.

Daily Wisdom for Women

A Narrow Gate

"For the gate is small and the way is narrow that leads to life."

MATTTHEW 7:14

It was time for the written driver's license renewal test. Having read the book from cover to cover and surviving the quizzing my husband initiated, I finally got my license. Knowing the right answers and then taking them to heart is critical in our spiritual life as well. You can't get to heaven unless you are truly born again.

One-Minute Meditations

False Prophets

"Beware of the false prophets, who come to you in sheep's clothing, but inwardly are ravenous wolves. You will know them by their fruits."

MATTHEW 7:15–16

God gave us a way to recognize the true teachers from the "wolves." "You will know them by their fruits." Those who abide in Christ preach that salvation comes to us by the grace of God, through the belief that Christ's blood has cleansed us from our sin.

Daily Wisdom for Women

A Furious Storm

"Save us, Lord; we are perishing!"

MATTHEW 8:25

Jesus took the disciples to the height of the storm's fury, yet He was with them. Later, Jesus rose up and rebuked the winds, and everything became calm. Yes, the storms of life will attempt to ravage me, but Christ is there, ready to deliver by just the power of His Word. He will carry me safely to the other side of the shore.

One-Minute Meditations

King Forever and Ever

*The L*ORD *is King forever and ever.*

PSALM 10:16

Satan has devoted all his efforts to eradicating Christianity. Yet, while the evil one's influence can seem ugly, Satan's mark on this earth will not be permanent. Jesus Christ lives forever within those who call upon His name. Jesus will remain King and will one day soon come back to claim this earth for His own, forever and ever.

Daily Wisdom for Women

The Lord Sees Us

*For the Lord is righteous,
He loves righteousness; the upright will behold His face.*

Psalm 11:7

Thanks to a judicial system that protects criminals, punishment for evil done upon the earth no longer seems to exist. But the wicked will pay for their deeds. Hell does exist.

The flip side of hell is heaven, the place where the righteous will behold His face. Where will you choose to spend eternity?

One-Minute Meditations

WHO ARE THE FAITHFUL?

*Help, LORD, for the godly man ceases to be,
for the faithful disappear from among the sons of men.*

PSALM 12:1

Who are the faithful? They are the ones who continue to follow God, no matter what obstacles are thrown in their path. They agree with Paul, that these present circumstances and trials are but "light and momentary" compared with the peace we will have in Christ for all eternity.

Daily Wisdom for Women

17 JANUARY

A Great Light

The people who walk in darkness will see a great light; those who live in a dark land, the light will shine on them.

Isaiah 9:2

Are you refusing to act on God's insight, insisting on pursuits that distract you from worshipping Him? How we spend our time is but a habit, and habits can be changed by repatterning our actions. Walk in the light, as your Father intended.

One-Minute Meditations

Our Advocate and Defender

*"Therefore everyone who confesses Me before men,
I will also confess him before My Father who is in heaven."*

MATTHEW 10:32

If we know Jesus Christ as Savior, Jesus remains forever our advocate before the Father, saying with love, "She's mine." Know that you are so precious to Jesus that He gave His life for you. Doesn't it feel incredible to have Jesus as your defender?

Daily Wisdom for Women

Joseph Honors God

*Now Joseph was well-built and handsome,
and after a while his master's wife took notice of Joseph and said,
"Come to bed with me!" But he refused.*

Genesis 39:6–8 NIV

A young woman told me the other day that the notion of celibacy before marriage is definitely passé. But for Joseph the very future of Israel teetered on his decision. Joseph's moral stand preserved the very ancestral line leading up to Jesus Christ.

One-Minute Meditations

20 JANUARY

Why Jesus Spoke in Parables

*And the disciples came and said to Him,
"Why do You speak to them in parables?"*

MATTHEW 13:10

Jesus Himself explains: "Therefore I speak to them in parables; because while seeing they do not see, and while hearing they do not hear, nor do they understand" (Matthew 13:13). Yet to those whom He knew would respond, He provided plain words. How open have you been to God's Word?

Daily Wisdom for Women

WISDOM COMES FROM GOD

*"Where did this man get this wisdom
and these miraculous powers?"*

MATTHEW 13:54

[Jesus] came from God, full of wisdom. Those who stood with Him during His earthly ministry had true wisdom and understanding from God. You obtain wisdom through a personal knowledge of Christ and by studying His Word. For only then can God's Spirit fill you with the wisdom you'll need to find and live out your God-given purpose.

One-Minute Meditations

22 JANUARY

RESCUED FROM MY ENEMIES

He reached down from on high and took hold of me;
he drew me out of deep waters. . . . The LORD was my support.

PSALM 18:16, 18 NIV

Have you ever known such desperation? Perhaps you were exactly where God wanted you, just as David was, and yet untold trials and tribulations were heaped on you anyway. When confronted with a crisis, like David, you can put your life in His hands.

Daily Wisdom for Women

So Much Promise

*"I will go down to Egypt with you,
and I will surely bring you back again."*

GENESIS 46:4 NIV

God promises to be with Jacob, giving him the assurance that he's not only in God's will but that God's presence will accompany him to this new homeland. The promises of the future will be filled with futility if God has not been given His rightful place in your home.

One-Minute Meditations

24 JANUARY

TRIALS HAVE A PURPOSE

*"Now do not be grieved or angry with yourselves,
because you sold me here, for God sent me before you to preserve life."*

GENESIS 45:5

Is there a hurt so deep inside that you have never shared it with another human being? Remember the pain suffered by Joseph. God knows your pain, and He is strong enough to remove any burden.

Daily Wisdom for Women

Of Little Faith

*"How is it that you do not understand that I did not
speak to you concerning bread? But beware of
the leaven of the Pharisees and Sadducees."*

MATTHEW 16:11

Jesus used a physical reality to get across a spiritual truth. His warning concerned the teachings of their religious leaders who knew the scriptures and yet denied Jesus as the Messiah. What miracle has Jesus accomplished in your life? And yet do you see with the eyes of faith who He really is?

One-Minute Meditations

JANUARY 26

A Life Turned Around

*"Who am I, that I should go to Pharaoh
and bring the Israelites out of Egypt?"*

EXODUS 3:11 NIV

When Moses asks God [this question] it comes from the heart of one who has murdered and knows his guilt before God. But instead of rebuke Moses hears, "I will be with you. . . . I am who I am" (Exodus 3:12, 14 NIV). This is the same "I Am" who calls you to serve Him today.

Daily Wisdom for Women

27 JANUARY

WHO IS CHRIST TO YOU?

*"But what about you?" he asked. "Who do you say I am?"
Simon Peter answered, "You are the Christ, the Son of the living God."*

MATTHEW 16:15–16 NIV

Jesus repeatedly asked this question to those who followed after Him. He knew that once He was gone, His followers would be scattered. It was crucial that they understood exactly who Christ was—Son of God, Son of man. Do you know Him as Savior?

One-Minute Meditations

28 JANUARY

Forsaken by God?

*My God, my God, why have You forsaken me?
Far from my deliverance are the words of my groaning.*

PSALM 22:1

Have you ever cried out to God with such despairing utterances as these? Jesus, separated from the Father because of our sin, experienced this that we would never be forsaken or walk alone the road which leads to Calvary. Where are you today? Walking toward Him? Sitting down bewildered? Or kneeling at His bleeding feet?

Daily Wisdom for Women

29 JANUARY

FIT FOR SERVICE

"Please, Lord. . .I am slow of speech and slow of tongue."
EXODUS 4:10

The Lord wanted Moses to understand that He could and would meet all of his needs. Moses needed to understand that God's power is limitless. Instead, Moses settled for allowing Aaron to speak for him.

Do you give the Lord part of your problem and then halfway through start solving it yourself?

One-Minute Meditations

30 JANUARY

Pharaoh Admits His Sin

"I have sinned this time; the LORD is the righteous one, and I and my people are the wicked ones."

Exodus 9:27

One would think that with an admission like this, [Pharaoh] had finally seen the light. However Pharaoh's heart had not yielded to God's authority. As soon as the storm passed, he refused to allow the Israelites to go. In the end his stubbornness would cause the loss of his son. This would be the final curse.

Daily Wisdom for Women

31 JANUARY

RENEWAL OF ALL THINGS

*"Truly I say to you, that you who have followed Me...
also shall sit upon twelve thrones, judging the twelve tribes of Israel."*

MATTHEW 19:28

Have you ever speculated as to what you might do in heaven? Don't worry, it's not going to be anything like what you've done on earth. The tasks you perform will be custom-tailored to you. "Job satisfaction" will finally fit into our vernacular.

One-Minute Meditations

1 FEBRUARY

Signs of a Scoundrel

*A scoundrel and villain, who goes about with a corrupt mouth,
who winks with his eye, signals with his feet and motions with his fingers,
who plots evil with deceit in his heart—he always stirs up dissension.*

PROVERBS 6:12–14 NIV

Modern-day charlatans may wear nice clothes. But underneath lies a destructive personality. Whom can we trust? The Ancient of Days, who always remains the same. He alone continues to guide and direct our paths.

Daily Wisdom for Women

2 FEBRUARY

The Passover Lamb

"Slay the Passover lamb.... And when He sees the blood on the lintel and on the two doorposts, the Lord will pass over the door and will not allow the destroyer to come in to your houses to smite you."

Exodus 12:21, 23

This scripture passage paints a comprehensive picture of the Passover. We can celebrate the Passover with joy and thanksgiving, knowing for certain that the long-awaited Messiah has come, and will come again!

One-Minute Meditations

3 FEBRUARY

A Pillar to Guide Them

Then they set out from Succoth and camped in Etham on the edge of the wilderness. The LORD was going before them in a pillar of cloud by day to lead them on the way, and in a pillar of fire by night to give them light, that they might travel by day and by night.

EXODUS 13:20–21

Finally the Israelites were on their way. As they left, their mighty God positioned Himself before them, leading them in a pillar of cloud. God was prepared. He's prepared today to move mountains for you.

Daily Wisdom for Women

FEBRUARY 4

An Invitation to Dine

"The kingdom of heaven may be compared to a king who gave a wedding feast for his son."

MATTHEW 22:2

When God sent His Son to earth, He invited all men and women to a wedding feast. Those who accept the invitation receive "wedding clothes." Jesus Christ now clothes them in His righteousness. Those not wearing these garments are cast out because they refused His salvation.

One-Minute Meditations

5 FEBRUARY

REMEMBER THE SABBATH

"Remember the sabbath day, to keep it holy."

EXODUS 20:8

In the very beginning of our marriage, my husband and I made a decision to honor God on Sunday. He has blessed our family over and over for this faithful commitment, providing not only the weekly spiritual guidance we desperately need, but also giving our bodies and souls the rest they require.

Daily Wisdom for Women

6 FEBRUARY

MOURNING TURNED INTO DANCING

Thou hast turned for me my mourning into dancing.

PSALM 30:11 KJV

Corrie ten Boom and her family were imprisoned in a Nazi death camp. Corrie alone survived that ordeal and went on to travel the world, sharing two messages: Jesus can turn loss into glory. And God's power of forgiveness turns mourning into dancing.

One-Minute Meditations

FEBRUARY 7

WISDOM CALLS OUT

Does not wisdom call, and understanding lift up her voice?
On top of the heights beside the way, where the paths meet,
she takes her stand; beside the gates, at the opening to the city,
at the entrance of the doors, she cries out.

PROVERBS 8:1–3

Wisdom calls to all of us, but some of us are just better listeners. Wisdom is a choice. We can walk right past it. Wisdom is at the very precipice of every decision.

Daily Wisdom for Women

8 FEBRUARY

Aaron's Priestly Robes

"And they shall make holy garments for Aaron your brother and his sons, that he may minister as priest to Me."

Exodus 28:4

The priests were appointed by God to minister directly to Him. God didn't want them to forget whom they served. As you come before the Lord today, in whatever garb and setting, reflect on these Old Testament times. Thank You, Jesus, for teaching us simply to talk to You.

One-Minute Meditations

9 FEBRUARY

Peter's Denial

*"Even though all may fall away because of You,
I will never fall away."*

MATTHEW 26:33

Peter was convinced that his faith in Christ was so strong nothing could cause it to crumble. Yet he openly denied his Lord. There have been times when you have disappointed Jesus. Have you asked for forgiveness? Have you realized that upon asking, the burden of sin will be lifted forever?

Daily Wisdom for Women

10 FEBRUARY

BEFORE HE SET THE HEAVENS IN PLACE

"The LORD possessed me at the beginning of His way, before His works of old."

PROVERBS 8:22

What existed before anything else? God. God designed, planned, and implemented all that we do see and everything we can't comprehend. He's still commanding the dawn to happen and the earth to keep spinning and the stars to remain in the sky. Aren't you glad?

One-Minute Meditations

11 FEBRUARY

OFFERINGS FOR THE TENT OF MEETING

Everyone who was willing and whose heart moved him came and brought an offering to the LORD.

EXODUS 35:21 NIV

When was the last time your whole community agreed on anything? Imagine everyone's talents, skills, and resources united for a common purpose! How is God using you in His church?

Daily Wisdom for Women

12 FEBRUARY

True Love Means Sacrifice

They spat on Him, and took the reed and began to beat Him on the head. After they had mocked Him, they took the scarlet robe off Him and put His own garments back on Him, and led Him away to crucify Him.

Matthew 27:30–31

To have done nothing wrong and to offer the ultimate sacrifice is an act only possible by God's Son. Jesus' offering of His body at Calvary gave eternal life to all who believe in Him.

One-Minute Meditations

13 FEBRUARY

The Spirit Confirms the Son

*He saw the heavens opening, and the Spirit
like a dove descending upon Him.*

MARK 1:10

John the Baptist prepared the people to recognize Christ when He came. And then Jesus Christ walked into Jordan to be baptized. As He came up out of the water, the Spirit of God descended on Him like a dove. "You are my Son, whom I love; with you I am well pleased" (Mark 1:11 NIV).

Daily Wisdom for Women

14 FEBRUARY

OFFERINGS TO THE LORD

"When any man of you brings an offering to the Lord, you shall bring your offering of animals from the herd or the flock."

LEVITICUS 1:2

God required proper and orderly worship. Only an unblemished male animal could be used as the burnt offering. There have not been any animal sacrifices since AD 70. Since Christ made His atoning sacrifice on the cross, our sins are forgiven based on His shed blood.

One-Minute Meditations

15 FEBRUARY

Peter's Mother-in-Law

And He came to her and raised her up, taking her by the hand, and the fever left her, and she waited on them.

MARK 1:31

Now here's Peter's mother-in-law sick in bed with a fever. Jesus tenderly takes the woman's hand and instantly heals her. Jesus meets every need for every situation if we come to Him in faith.

Daily Wisdom for Women

16 FEBRUARY

A Woman of Folly

The woman of folly is boisterous, she is naive and knows nothing. She sits at the doorway of her house, on a seat by the high places of the city, calling to those who pass by.

PROVERBS 9:13–15

Have you ever felt like this woman? Did you start out with endless options and then begin purchasing tickets to oblivion? With Christ it's not too late to cash in that pass to nowhere.

With Christ your life will have direction.

One-Minute Meditations

FEBRUARY 17

Jesus' Earthly Family Reacts

Answering them, He said, "Who are My mother and My brothers?...
For whoever does the will of God, he is My brother and sister and mother."

Mark 3:33, 35

As women, are we using our precious moments to further the gospel, or are we involved in trivial pursuits? Do we stand alongside those in our families who dare to make a difference? Or have we added to their burdens by missing their obvious purpose?

Daily Wisdom for Women

18 FEBRUARY

TO TOUCH JESUS' CLOAK

"If I just touch His garments, I will get well."
MARK 5:28

This woman is frantic. In one last-ditch effort she reaches out to touch the garment of Jesus as He passes by. "Immediately Jesus. . .turned around in the crowd and said, 'Who touched My garments?' " (Mark 5:30) The disciples think He's "losing it" for sure.

"But the woman. . .aware of what had happened to her, came. . .and told Him the whole truth" (Mark 5:33). Does your faith shine through even in small gestures?

One-Minute Meditations

19 FEBRUARY

The Lord's Diet Plan

"These are the creatures which you may eat from all the animals that are on the earth."

Leviticus 11:2

Since Moses was chosen by God to deliver these dietary restrictions to the Israelites, we can imagine the response he received. In those days, if the Israelites hadn't obeyed God's dietary laws most of them would have died from food poisoning. God was preserving the nation from which the Messiah would be born.

Daily Wisdom for Women

20 FEBRUARY

Happy Birthday

I will give thanks to You, for I am fearfully and wonderfully made.
PSALM 139:14

I don't know the date of your birthday, but this one is mine. So celebrate with me today, keeping thoughts of your own special day in mind. God rejoiced at your birth. You were fashioned exactly the way He wanted you. How incredible to comprehend that, when you awake in the morning, God is already thinking about you! (Psalm 139:17–18).

One-Minute Meditations

21 FEBRUARY

U-Hauls Don't Follow Hearses

*Behold, You have made my days as handbreadths,
and my lifetime as nothing in Your sight;
surely every man at his best is a mere breath.*

PSALM 39:5

God wants us to trust Him for our future. To know our lifespan would affect us every day of our life. So God has guarded this secret as a great favor to us. To worry about the future is to be uncertain of your eternity.

Daily Wisdom for Women

February 22

The Wise of Heart

*The wise of heart will receive commands,
but a babbling fool will be ruined. He who walks in integrity
walks securely, but he who perverts his ways will be found out.*

Proverbs 10:8–9

My repeated prayer for all our children was this: "Lord, protect them and surround them with Your angels. And if they're disobedient, let them be found out." Is there a young person in your life who needs your prayers today?

One-Minute Meditations

23 FEBRUARY

Jesus Drives Out a Demon

As soon as she heard about him, a woman whose little daughter was possessed by an evil spirit came and fell at his feet.

Mark 7:25 NIV

Even during the time of Christ, diabolic forces knew no age barriers. Jesus came to bring the Good News to the Jews first. But this woman, a Gentile, says she needs Jesus' touch, too. And He responds to her faith. Ask Jesus to touch your life this day.

Daily Wisdom for Women

24 FEBRUARY

COMMANDMENTS OR SUGGESTIONS?

*"You shall keep My statutes and practice them;
I am the Lord who sanctifies you."*

LEVITICUS 20:8

When God gave the Laws to Moses, He expected them to be observed. They were commandments, not "suggestions." Our hope lies in the fact that Jesus Christ has paid the penalty for all our sin on Calvary's cross. "But if we confess our sins to him, He is faithful and just to forgive us" (1 John 1:9 NLT).

One-Minute Meditations

25 FEBRUARY

Jesus Is Transfigured

*And He was transfigured before them;
and His garments became radiant and exceedingly white.*

Mark 9:2–3

Christ performs the miracle of metamorphosis in us when we come to believe in Him as Lord and Savior. He transforms us, quickening our spirits, so that we are destined to spend eternity with God in heaven. It's a change on the inside which is displayed on the outside—for the unbelieving world to see.

Daily Wisdom for Women

26 FEBRUARY

Is It Lawful to Divorce?

"For this reason a man shall leave his father and mother, and the two shall become one flesh; so they are no longer two, but one flesh. What therefore God has joined together, let no man separate."

Mark 10:7–9

"Divorce is like trying to pull apart two pieces of paper which have been glued together for years and years. It's impossible to do this without tearing them both apart." God wants to bless your marriage.

One-Minute Meditations

27 FEBRUARY

THE YEAR OF JUBILEE

"You shall have the fiftieth year as a jubilee; you shall not sow, nor reap its aftergrowth, nor gather in from its untrimmed vines."

LEVITICUS 25:11

Are you scratching your head, wondering why on earth this passage is here? Every fiftieth year God arranged a wonderful, year-long celebration—a jubilee—for His chosen people, the Israelites.

God's ways are filled with wisdom. If only the world would realize His majesty!

Daily Wisdom for Women

28 FEBRUARY

In Memory of the Righteous

The memory of the righteous is blessed, but the name of the wicked will rot.

PROVERBS 10:7

[A mother's] parting admonition to the children who gathered around her deathbed was "be good and love each other." And then her Lord peacefully escorted her to the mansion He'd prepared. To leave a rich legacy of love, one must be dearly acquainted with the Author of Love, our heavenly Father.

One-Minute Meditations

1 MARCH

JESUS PROPHESIES HIS DEATH

"They will mock Him and spit on Him, and scourge Him and kill Him, and three days later He will rise again."

MARK 10:34

Christ's disciples couldn't cope with the thought of His leaving and therefore became fearful. Jesus gently encouraged them with the hope of His resurrection. When grief overwhelms us, let us remember [Christ's] death on Calvary's cross provides our hope of eternal life in heaven.

Daily Wisdom for Women

2 MARCH

God Orders a Census

*"Take a census of all the congregation of the sons of Israel. . . .
You and Aaron shall number them by their armies."*

Numbers 1:2–3

The Israelites needed to know the strength of their army. So God showed Moses a way to determine this.

Notice that men were to serve Israel's army from the time they were twenty years old. In doing so, they would be preserving their nation to the time when Messiah would be born.

One-Minute Meditations

3 MARCH

By Whose Authority Did Jesus Act?

"By what authority are You doing these things, or who gave You this authority to do these things?"

MARK 11:28

This is the kind of squeeze play the Pharisees and scribes tried constantly to force Jesus into. No matter what Jesus said, He'd be wrong. And yet this tactic always backfired on them. Jesus Christ cannot be fooled. He knew the hearts of the Pharisees and scribes, and He knows your heart, too.

Daily Wisdom for Women

4 MARCH

Never Take a Drink?

*"When a man or woman makes a special vow. . .
to dedicate himself to the Lord,
he shall abstain from wine and strong drink."*

NUMBERS 6:2–3

Drinking liquor had a negative effect on my emotions. When I became a Christian, drinking was the first thing to go. I refused to provide a breeding ground in which this substance might interfere with the plans God desired for my life and future. The Lord has remained faithful to provide all the inspiration I need.

One-Minute Meditations

5 MARCH

BEWARE OF THE SCRIBES

In His teaching He was saying: "Beware of the scribes...
who devour widows' houses, and for appearance's sake offer long prayers;
these will receive greater condemnation."

MARK 12:38, 40

All of us are responsible not only to read the Word of God with understanding but also to have discernment concerning the clergy who minister to us. Is their primary goal to make sure their flock is ultimately led to God's glory?

Daily Wisdom for Women

6 MARCH

Walking in the Light of God's Goodness

*The righteous will never be shaken,
but the wicked will not dwell in the land.*

PROVERBS 10:30

Knowing that everything which emanates from God is good enables us to trust Him. In each situation there are two alternative reactions. On the one hand exists the opportunity to act honorably, and on the other freedom to disobey. Obedience always brings inner peace, while stepping out from underneath God's umbrella of protection only gets us saturated with sin.

One-Minute Meditations

7 MARCH

Sinners from Birth

*Behold, I was brought forth in iniquity,
and in sin my mother conceived me.*

PSALM 51:5

David spoke from the depths of his broken heart. He had viewed the lovely Bathsheba as she prepared to bathe. Hypnotized by her beauty he "took her." Admitting our own sinful state is the first step toward a more sincere Christian walk. And acknowledging the sin in our children makes us more effective Christian parents.

Daily Wisdom for Women

8 MARCH

Sibling Rivalry

*Then the Lord. . .called. . .Miriam.
"Why then were you not afraid to speak against
My servant, against Moses?"*

Numbers 12:5, 8

How could [Miriam] even think of asking God to explain Himself? But don't we all do the same thing? How about, "If there's a God then why is there suffering?" God is not responsible for our sin. The power to make a choice between good and evil is a gift from God. What we do is up to us.

One-Minute Meditations

9 MARCH

When Fear Paralyzes

*A young man was following Him, wearing nothing but
a linen sheet over his naked body; and they seized him. . . .
They led Jesus away to the high priest.*

MARK 14:51, 53

You awake to the sound of the doorknob being turned. What do you do? John Mark escaped the threatening situation. Jesus Christ remained in the eye of the storm, yet in perfect sync with the Father. When fear paralyzes, help is only a prayer away.

Daily Wisdom for Women

10 MARCH

THE CHALLENGE OF KORAH

Now Korah. . .said. . ."You have gone far enough, for all the congregation are holy. . .so why do you exalt yourselves above the assembly of the Lord?"

NUMBERS 16:1, 3

Korah didn't want to be called a sinner. He opted to pretend this fight for control existed between him and Moses instead of between him and God. Do you fight for control of your life? Surrender the ultimate control to God and realize the freedom of His perfect plan.

One-Minute Meditations

11 MARCH

Barabbas Is Released

*But the chief priests stirred up the crowd
to ask him to release Barabbas.*

MARK 15:11

The priests were but players in the great drama prophesied hundreds of years earlier in the Old Testament. Jesus Christ would be sentenced to death by Pilate, even though Pilate found Him without guilt. Jesus Christ must die for the sins of humankind. Today we know the truth. And we can share, without fear, without guilt, the kingship of Jesus Christ.

Daily Wisdom for Women

12 MARCH

JOSEPH OF ARIMATHEA

Joseph of Arimathea came. . .and he gathered up courage and went in before Pilate, and asked for the body of Jesus.

MARK 15:43

Joseph, present during the sessions in which the Council members solidified decisions concerning Christ, never consented to their plan of action. Nicodemus also stood his ground. These men had been born again through their faith in Christ. And knowing the scriptures concerning the death of their Savior, they prepared for it.

One-Minute Meditations

13 MARCH

The Red Heifer

*"Then the heifer shall be burned in his sight;
its hide and its flesh and its blood, with its refuse, shall be burned."*

Numbers 19:5

Animal sacrifices will begin again when the Antichrist comes on the scene. He will use such sacrifices to mimic God Almighty and demand worship for himself.

Are you remaining in the Word? The days ahead demand that we be knowledgeable women, filled with the understanding of Jesus Christ.

Daily Wisdom for Women

14 MARCH

WHERE DO YOU TAKE REFUGE?

*In God I have put my trust; I shall not be afraid,
What can mere man do to me?*

PSALM 56:4

David wrote this when the Philistines had seized him. He called upon his God to deliver him, and the Lord prevailed. Where do you go for refuge? I run to the arms of my loving Father, just as David did in his own crisis. And He always comes through.

One-Minute Meditations

15 MARCH

John the Baptist Is Born

*But they had no child, because Elizabeth was barren,
and they were both advanced in years.*

LUKE 1:7

One day, as he offered incense before the altar, an angel of the Lord appeared and said, "Do not be afraid, Zacharias, for your petition has been heard, and your wife Elizabeth will bear you a son, and you will give him the name John" (Luke 1:13). This was God's perfect plan, the fulfillment of His promises.

Daily Wisdom for Women

16 MARCH

God's Deterrent to Sin

*"Take all the leaders of the people and execute them
in broad daylight before the Lord, so that the fierce anger
of the Lord may turn away from Israel."*

Numbers 25:4

If you're a parent, you probably devote much time and energy to keeping your children from getting involved in things that would harm them. In the same way, God, our loving parent, must pull in the reins when people drift too far from His truth.

One-Minute Meditations

17 MARCH

Anna, the Prophetess

And there was a prophetess, Anna. . . . She never left the temple, serving night and day with fastings and prayers.

Luke 2:36–37

Anna had faithfully served in the temple her entire life. And God had promised that she would see the Messiah before she died. She waited eighty-four years. And He kept His Word. Let us strive to follow Anna's prayerful example, and we, too, will be blessed by God.

Daily Wisdom for Women

18 MARCH

God Gave Israel the Land

*Then the Lord spoke to Moses, saying,
"Among these the land shall be divided for an inheritance."*

NUMBERS 26:52–53

God picked for Himself a people. And He blessed them with this land as an inheritance.

One day Christ will return to claim the Holy Land for His people. Christ is coming back as the ultimate Judge and Rescuer of Israel. The time is now to be sure of our commitment to Christ.

One-Minute Meditations

19 MARCH

One Calling in the Desert

*And he came into all the district around the Jordan,
preaching a baptism of repentance for the forgiveness of sins.*

Luke 3:3

Counting on their heritage as a means of automatic salvation, the religious leaders called themselves Abraham's children. Yet to be Abraham's children required that they display faith. John's exhortations were aimed at the "wilderness of men's souls." How many churchgoers do you know who claim the faith yet exist in a wasteland of sin?

Daily Wisdom for Women

20 MARCH

A Refuge from Our Despair

*Hear my cry, O God. . . . From the end of the earth I call to You. . .
for You have been a refuge for me.*

PSALM 61:1–3

David clung with tenacity to the fact that no matter how desperate his situation appeared, God was as immovable as a boulder. Although David's trials may differ from yours, you, too, can use strong coping mechanisms.

First, acknowledge God remains all powerful. Second, look back at God's past rescues.

One-Minute Meditations

21 MARCH

The Israelites Leave Egypt

The sons of Israel. . .journeyed from Rameses in the first month, on the fifteenth day of the first month.

Numbers 33:1, 3

God inspired Moses to write the accounts of the trials of the Israelites, where they traveled, and the events which transpired. At times, their hardships made them long to be back in bondage in Egypt. But much of their pain was because they refused to obey.

Daily Wisdom for Women

22 MARCH

Why Mary and Joseph Married

"Every daughter who comes into possession of an inheritance of any tribe of the sons of Israel shall be wife to one of the family of the tribe of her father."

Numbers 36:8

Mary and Joseph married because they loved each other but more importantly, both of them loved God and desired to be a part of His purpose for man. And within this environment of submission, Israel's inheritance, the Savior, remained secure.

One-Minute Meditations

23 MARCH

Jesus Is Tempted by Satan

And the devil said to Him, "If You are the Son of God, tell this stone to become bread."

Luke 4:3

Have you ever found yourself so tempted that you ached? Christ understands. In this first temptation, Satan intimated that there must be something wrong with the Father's love for the Son since He allowed Him to go hungry. Second, Satan attempted to get Christ to bypass the cross. The third temptation questioned the Father's faithfulness.

Daily Wisdom for Women

24 MARCH

Shout for Joy

*Shout joyfully to God, all the earth;
sing the glory of His name; make His praise glorious.*

Psalm 66:1–2

When pondering Jesus as the friend of sinners, the lion of the tribe of Judah, or the Alpha and Omega, your mind focuses on Him and daily problems diminish.

David knew even in his day that taking time to praise his awesome God provided strength and renewal for his weary soul. Joyfully he worshipped!

One-Minute Meditations

25 MARCH

Matthew, the Tax Collector

*He said to him, "Follow Me." And he left everything behind,
and got up and began to follow Him.
And Levi gave a big reception for Him in his house.*

Luke 5:27–29

Levi (Matthew) responded to Christ's invitation to follow Him. Christ's presence at the reception provided an opportunity for Him to share the gospel message. We, too, can seek out those whom society shuns and offer the compassion of Christ.

Daily Wisdom for Women

26 MARCH

MOSES APPOINTS JUDGES

"Choose wise and discerning and experienced men from your tribes, and I will appoint them as your heads."

DEUTERONOMY 1:13

God demands trust from His people and His spiritual leaders.

Now that their wandering days were over, Moses charged these twelve tribal officials to judge fairly the disputes among the people. They were about to take possession of the land God had promised them. Do you trust God for everything?

One-Minute Meditations

27 MARCH

BEFORE CHOOSING THE TWELVE

He spent the whole night in prayer to God.
And when day came, He called His disciples to Him.

LUKE 6:12–13

Christ prayed all night for the men who would preach, teach, heal the sick, raise the dead, and record His Words. Christ chose a solitary spot, minimizing His distractions. When it's time to do battle, we need to be alone first. Then, after we know God's will, we can solicit the prayers of others.

Daily Wisdom for Women

28 MARCH

A FATHER TO THE FATHERLESS

A father of the fatherless. . .is God in His holy habitation.

PSALM 68:5

What can we do to ensure that our children aren't among the fatherless? We can make sure that we are fully committed to the Lord. God has promised to be "a father of the fatherless." Count on Him to keep His Word. And instead of attempting to be both father and mother, you can just be a mom to your kids.

One-Minute Meditations

29 MARCH

Our Triune God

"Hear, O Israel! The LORD is our God, the LORD is one!"

DEUTERONOMY 6:4

When God speaks of Himself, the plural pronoun is used: "Then God said, 'Let Us make man in Our image, according to Our likeness'" (Genesis 1:26). All three persons of the Trinity were present. Only God could have omnisciently conceived of the Trinity. God has always been, and will forever be.

Daily Wisdom for Women

30 MARCH

THE ORIGINAL "ME GENERATION"

And He sent them out to proclaim the kingdom of God.

LUKE 9:2

[Christ] instructed His apostles not to take any provisions with them. Jesus wanted them to learn to rely fully on Him. They had been with Christ on a daily basis, learning how to reach out with compassion. Instead they displayed both selfishness and a lack of love. Yet they were God's Plan A.

One-Minute Meditations

31 MARCH

A Call to Holiness

There shall not be found among you. . .one who practices witchcraft.
DEUTERONOMY 18:10

Our sons easily tire of most board games. But they became fascinated after one of their friends introduced them to the game "Dungeons and Dragons."

About the same time, our church encouraged high schoolers to sign up for the seminar "Basic Youth Conflicts." All the way home our son spoke about how the game had usurped the time he used to spend with the Lord. He [then] burned every one of the game's expensive books. From that moment Jeff never looked back.

Is God receiving all the glory in your life?

Daily Wisdom for Women

1 APRIL

Moses Is in Glory

And they were Moses and Elijah, who, appearing in glory, were speaking of His departure which He was about to accomplish at Jerusalem.

LUKE 9:30–31

We are not now what we will become. Whether we die or are taken up by the Rapture, the Lord will someday allow this "earth suit" of ours to fall away and issue us our "eternity suit."

In spite of your life, are you assured of your salvation?

One-Minute Meditations

2 APRIL

A Rock of Refuge

*Be to me a rock of habitation to which I may continually come;
You have given commandment to save me,
for You are my rock and my fortress.*

PSALM 71:3

I considered another Psalm about the rock. "Be to me a rock of strength, a stronghold to save me" (Psalm 31:2). Over fifty times in scripture, the word *rock* is used in reference to God. When everything else fails, He is steadfast, immovable, and unchangeable.

Daily Wisdom for Women

3 APRIL

WHY DO WE HAVE DROUGHT?

But it shall come about, if you do not obey the LORD your God. . . all these curses will come upon you.

DEUTERONOMY 28:15

Shortly after the Northridge, California, quake in 1994, the newspaper carried a nearly hidden tidbit of information. The triangle formed by the three cities hardest hit by the temblor was the epicenter for nearly seventy companies which crank out more than 95 percent of the pornographic videos made in the United States. God's power cannot be denied.

One-Minute Meditations

4 APRIL

Martha and Mary

*She had a sister called Mary,
who was seated at the Lord's feet, listening to His word.
But Martha was distracted with all her preparations.*

LUKE 10:39–40

Who knew better than Christ how to put the pressures of life into perspective? He had only three years to establish His ministry, train His disciples, and present the gospel. Yet we see no record of Him hurrying others.

Have you taken time to get to know your Lord?

Daily Wisdom for Women

5 APRIL

CIRCUMCISION OF THE HEART

"Moreover the LORD your God will circumcise your heart and the heart of your descendants, to love the LORD your God with all your heart and with all your soul."

DEUTERONOMY 30:6

Today's scripture recalls when God called the Israelites to be circumcised. This physical cutting away of the foreskin symbolized that they were God's own. God would someday perform a circumcision on their hearts as well.

Does your heart need a checkup?

One-Minute Meditations

6 APRIL

The Lord of Parables

Listen, O my people, to my instruction; incline your ears to the words of my mouth. I will open my mouth in a parable.

Psalm 78:1–2

Sometimes Jesus offered His perfect insight in parables. He knew that those whose hearts were open and receptive to Him would understand its meaning. On the other hand, those whose hearts held only self-righteousness would not understand even if He spoke plainly.

Is your heart ready to listen to Jesus?

Daily Wisdom for Women

7 APRIL

Joshua Is Chosen

"Be strong and courageous, for you shall go with this people into the land which the LORD has sworn to their fathers to give them."

DEUTERONOMY 31:7

Moses, who is preparing to die, names Joshua as his successor. Right there, in the presence of all Israel, Moses admonishes Joshua to "be strong and courageous." God chose Joshua because he had faithfully served Moses throughout all their years in the wilderness.

One-Minute Meditations

8 APRIL

The Unforgivable Sin

"But he who denies Me before men will be denied before the angels of God."

LUKE 12:9

All men need a Savior. And the Bible states clearly that "There is salvation in no one else; for there is no other name under heaven that has been given among men by which we must be saved" (Acts 4:12). Jesus Christ is that Savior.

If you refuse to be "born again," you will not be received in heaven.

Daily Wisdom for Women

9 APRIL

SPARE THE ROD

*He who withholds his rod hates his son,
but he who loves him disciplines him diligently.*

PROVERBS 13:24

I discovered that the fastest way to redirect my children's beastly actions was to require an immediate kindness as retribution to the injured party. I understood that discipline is meant to teach the correct behavior. Punishment only makes a child bitter.

One-Minute Meditations

10 APRIL

A Willing Heart

"How often I have longed to gather your children together, as a hen gathers her chicks under her wings, but you were not willing!"

LUKE 13:34 NIV

How like the Israelites I am! God showed them the path they were to walk in. He even defined the boundaries for them. And yet time after time they leaped beyond the lines of safety and tried to live without Him.

Is it time for you to let God steer the course?

Daily Wisdom for Women

11 APRIL

A Smooth Transition

Now Joshua. . .was filled with the spirit of wisdom, for Moses had laid his hands on him; and the sons of Israel listened to him and did as the Lord had commanded Moses.

Deuteronomy 34:9

Our God has a perfect sense of order. God had spoken with Moses, and Moses instructed the people to follow Joshua.

Has God been trying to lead you somewhere, and you haven't followed?

One-Minute Meditations

12 APRIL

The God of Our Salvation

Help us, O God of our salvation, for the glory of Your name; and deliver us and forgive our sins for Your name's sake.

Psalm 79:9

Have you ever cried out to God for deliverance, recognizing that your own circumstances are a result of leaving the Lord out of the decision making? But God's not surprised. He's not only aware of what you've done, He watched you make this awful choice and witnessed the harm you did.

Daily Wisdom for Women

13 APRIL

The Holocaust Revisited

*"Come," they say, "let us destroy them as a nation,
that the name of Israel be remembered no more."*

PSALM 83:4 NIV

Schindler's List provided a fresh reminder not only of what the Jews suffered during World War II, but that only a remnant survived these atrocities.

In this Psalm, David reveals the sinister plot to wipe out those whom the Lord cherishes. For this reason, the Lord has placed the archangel Michael in charge of Israel's protection (Daniel 10:21).

One-Minute Meditations

14 APRIL

God Uses Rahab

"Go, view the land, especially Jericho." So they went and came into the house of a harlot whose name was Rahab, and lodged there.

JOSHUA 2:1

When the king of Jericho found out that two Israelites had sneaked into town, he sent word to Rahab, saying, "Bring out the men who have come to you" (Joshua 2:3).

Instead, Rahab hid Joshua's men on her roof, then requested that her life and her family be delivered from death.

Daily Wisdom for Women

15 APRIL

Taxes Must Be Paid

*Every person is to be in subjection to the governing authorities.
For there is no authority except from God. . . .
For because of this you also pay taxes,
for rulers are servants of God.*

Romans 13:1, 6

Governments are established by God. Know that they are accountable to God. Have you finished filling out your IRS forms? Let's reassure each other that our money isn't being thrown away. We're following scripture. . .we're supporting a government that God has blessed.

One-Minute Meditations

16 APRIL

WHEN EVERYONE IN HEAVEN REJOICES

*" 'Rejoice with me, for I have found the coin which I had lost!'
In the same way, I tell you, there is joy in the presence of
the angels of God over one sinner who repents."*

LUKE 15:9–10

Jesus compared the woman's joy to the celebration in heaven when a sinner repents and "Son-beams" of peace finally flood into the soul. It's the feeling of wholeness a person hungers for all her life.

Daily Wisdom for Women

17 APRIL

Heaven or Hell?

*"In Hades he lifted up his eyes, being in torment,
and saw Abraham far away and Lazarus in his bosom."*

Luke 16:23

In life each man chose the final direction his soul would take. After death both are totally aware of the great chasm that exists between them. Once life has ceased, we no longer have the power to change our eternal destination. Although he suffered in life, the poor man now resided in paradise.

One-Minute Meditations

18 APRIL

Twelve Stones

"Take up for yourselves twelve stones from here out of the middle of the Jordan. . .and carry them over with you and lay them down in the lodging place where you will lodge tonight."

JOSHUA 4:3

Standing on the other side of the Jordan River, the men of Israel now followed God's command. These stones represented each of the tribes of Israel. Piled up high, they produced a visible monument as to the miracle God performed.

Daily Wisdom for Women

19 APRIL

A Blast of Terror

"Truly I say to you, whoever does not receive the kingdom of God like a child will not enter it at all."

MARK 10:15

We watched the firefighter carry the body of Baylee Almon away from the Oklahoma City bomb site, and sighed, "Not that precious baby, Lord!" When Christ was born, King Herod ordered that all male children in Bethlehem be slaughtered. Was their grief less than the suffering of those in Oklahoma City? I think not.

One-Minute Meditations

20 APRIL

Circle of Fear

The Lord said to Joshua, "See, I have given Jericho into your hand, with its king and the valiant warriors."

Joshua 6:2

God gave the Israelites an elaborate battle plan and led them all in battle! And this is the same Lord who is waiting for you to come to Him each and every day. He's waiting to lift you higher than you ever thought possible.

Daily Wisdom for Women

21 APRIL

Rebuke the Sinner

"Be on your guard! If your brother sins, rebuke him; and if he repents, forgive him."

Luke 17:3

It still takes the knowledge of Jesus Christ to redeem our world. Here Jesus admonished his disciples to "rebuke" their brothers if they've sinned. Sin is a progressive fall. "Real love" means intervening that we might get back on track.

Have you shared your love of Jesus? Pray that God might open a door to your witness.

One-Minute Meditations

22 APRIL

LIVING WITH A VIEW OF HEAVEN

My soul longed and even yearned for the courts of the LORD.

PSALM 84:2

King David had an eternal perspective. Israel constantly battled its enemies. How he must have longed for a lasting peace. But he had to settle for that little niche of peace he carved out for himself while pondering what heaven was like, anticipating the day he'd dwell with God. For the God of perfection created for Himself a place of eternal security.

Daily Wisdom for Women

23 APRIL

JESUS PREPARES HIS DISCIPLES

"Behold, we are going up to Jerusalem, and all things which are written through the prophets about the Son of Man will be accomplished."

LUKE 18:31

As His time on earth drew to its inevitable close, Jesus began preparing His disciples for the time when He'd be gone from them. He needed to help them accept His death, understand the reason for it. What is Jesus saying to you?

One-Minute Meditations

24 APRIL

The Sun Stood Still

*So the sun stood still, and the moon stopped,
until the nation avenged themselves of their enemies.*

Joshua 10:13

Five kings banded together, aligning themselves against the Israelites, but God gave Joshua victory over the Amorites by causing huge hailstones to rain down from heaven. Meanwhile, the five kings sought refuge in a cave. If God is able to stop the solar system, He is able to deal with every crisis in your life.

Daily Wisdom for Women

25 APRIL

True and Lasting Justice

"In a certain city there was a judge who did not fear God and did not respect man."

Luke 18:2

Back in New Testament times, judges held court in a traveling tent. This widow already had three strikes against her. As a woman, as a widow, and without the funds to pay for assistance, she was without hope. If you've been denied justice here on earth, you have a God who knows all. Justice will be served!

One-Minute Meditations

26 APRIL

Carefully Choosing Our Words

The one who guards his mouth preserves his life;
the one who opens wide his lips comes to ruin.

Proverbs 13:3

As this proverb points out, the very words we speak denote the depth of our character. Each day presents an opportunity to extend to others words that reach in to soothe and heal souls—or deepen wounds.

Daily Wisdom for Women

27 APRIL

Idols of Their Own Making

*Among the gods there is none like you,
O Lord; no deeds can compare with yours. . . .
For you are great and do marvelous deeds; you alone are God.*

PSALM 86:8, 10 NIV

We were all created with a "God-shaped void" inside our souls. The purpose of this void is to draw us to the Lord in commitment.

God is constantly guiding us in our search for knowledge and understanding.

One-Minute Meditations

28 APRIL

God Instructs Joshua

Now these are the territories which the sons of Israel inherited in the land of Canaan, which Eleazar the priest, and Joshua the son of Nun. . .apportioned to them for an inheritance.

JOSHUA 14:1

Caleb [went] into battle, driving out the sons of Anak, but Joseph's sons failed to drive out the Canaanites. And because Israel failed to drive out their enemies completely, there has been conflict in the Middle East ever since.

Daily Wisdom for Women

29 APRIL

Riding on a Donkey

*"Go into the village ahead of you;
there, as you enter, you will find a colt tied on which
no one yet has ever sat; untie it and bring it here."*

LUKE 19:30

Jesus came to them, riding on a donkey. The reason is that He might present Himself to them as their humble servant and king. If He had ridden into Jerusalem on a horse, He would have presented Himself as a warrior.

One-Minute Meditations

30 APRIL

HERE COMES THE JUDGE

Now it came about after the death of Joshua that the sons of Israel inquired of the LORD, saying, "Who shall go up first for us against the Canaanites, to fight against them?"

JUDGES 1:1

All the days of Joshua's life, Israel had served the Lord. The next generation had no direct dealings with God and walked away from Him, plunging Israel into many years of spiritual darkness. These are the days of the judges.

Daily Wisdom for Women

1 MAY

In the Beginning, Christ

*In the beginning was the Word,
and the Word was with God, and the Word was God.*

John 1:1

The church [Esther] attended was a cult of false teachers. These teachers said Jesus Christ did not exist in the flesh but was instead spirit.

True believers know differently: "Every spirit that confesses that Jesus Christ has come in the flesh is from God; and every spirit that does not confess Jesus is not from God" (1 John 4:2–3).

One-Minute Meditations

2 MAY

Music in the Morning

*It is good to give thanks to the Lord
and to sing praises to Your name.*

Psalm 92:1

This particular Psalm was actually written for a Sabbath celebration. If you ever attend a Messianic service, you'll discover that believers in Yeshua definitely have the market cornered on celebrating. It's the kind of merriment God designed for us to enjoy with Him. And it's probably the closest reenactment of heavenly worship you'll find on this earth.

Daily Wisdom for Women

3 MAY

THE WISE WOMAN BUILDS HER HOUSE

*The wise woman builds her house,
but the foolish tears it down with her own hands.*

PROVERBS 14:1

Every woman must understand God's "building codes" in order to strengthen her own household. The blueprints must be followed. From these a concrete foundation is laid. Likewise, how can a woman provide guidance within her home unless she first seeks wisdom from the Lord?

One-Minute Meditations

4 MAY

He Dwelt among Us

*And the Word became flesh,
and dwelt among us, and we saw His glory.*

JOHN 1:14

That phrase, "dwelt among us," means God took on the form of a human body and came to earth to become a model for men and women.

This is what Christ purchased for us on Calvary's cross: the right to be indwelt with the very Spirit of God.

Daily Wisdom for Women

5 MAY

ISRAEL BREAKS THE COVENANT

"But you have not obeyed Me."

JUDGES 2:2

No sooner had the Israelites taken possession of their land than they forgot all the Lord's admonitions.

God's hand was now against them for choosing to worship idols instead of honoring Him. Discipline was required to bring them back. So God left five enemy nations as strongholds within the region to test Israel's obedience to His commandments.

One-Minute Meditations

6 MAY

A Discerning Woman

Wisdom reposes in the heart of the discerning and even among fools she lets herself be known.

PROVERBS 14:33 NIV

Dorothy attended my Bible study group each week. From her perspective, the word *cherish* didn't exist in her husband's vocabulary.

We would pray over her marriage and then she'd play a beautiful hymn on the piano. How well Dorothy understood this [proverb]. Although she couldn't change her husband's heart, her own was filled with wisdom.

Daily Wisdom for Women

7 MAY

Israel Enslaved Again

The Lord strengthened Eglon the king of Moab against Israel, because they had done evil in the sight of the Lord.

JUDGES 3:12

The Israelites again fell into idol worship. Therefore, Eglon, king of Moab, overpowered Israel, and took possession of the city of palms. They were now forced to serve the king of one of their enemies for eighteen years. Finally, they cried out for deliverance and the Lord sent Ehud. Peace reigned for eighty years.

One-Minute Meditations

8 MAY

The Gift of Manna

*They asked, and He brought quail,
and satisfied them with the bread of heaven.*

PSALM 105:40

Life-giving bread is symbolically offered to us under the new covenant. Jesus said, "I am the living bread that came down out of heaven; if anyone eats of this bread, he will live forever; and the bread also which I will give for the life of the world is My flesh" (John 6:51).

Daily Wisdom for Women

9 MAY

Elijah Will Come

*They asked him, "What then? Are you Elijah?"
And he said, "I am not."*

JOHN 1:21

Clearly, John answers the Jews, saying that he is not Elijah. However, he did come in the spirit and power of Elijah and even dressed as Elijah had. John preached a message of judgment for the religious leaders of Israel, who should have both known and understood the Word of God but refused to listen.

One-Minute Meditations

10 MAY

MOTIVES OF THE HEART

*Commit your works to the L*ORD *and your plans will be established.*

PROVERBS 16:3

Surrounding us are beings [that] belong to Satan. Their purpose is to seduce us into wavering from the truth. They dangle us from the scaffolding of unbelief. Did God mean what He said? Do we really need Him telling us what to do? Absolutely! Only God can give us an eternal future in heaven with Him.

Daily Wisdom for Women

11 MAY

DEBORAH, JUDGE AND PROPHETESS

Now Deborah. . .used to sit under the palm tree of Deborah. . . and the sons of Israel came up to her for judgment.

JUDGES 4:4–5

Deborah is best known for her mediating role in Israel's great battle against King Jabin of Canaan.

The commander of Jabin's army was Sisera. With his nine hundred iron chariots, he oppressed the sons of Israel for twenty years. The time had come for Israel's liberation.

Is the Lord on your side, too?

One-Minute Meditations

12 MAY

DEBORAH TRUSTS GOD

*"Arise! For this is the day in which the Lord
has given Sisera into your hands."*

JUDGES 4:14

Barak knew that he'd have to take God at His Word.

Barak and his troops chased the enemy, killing them all. Then Barak backtracked to search for Sisera, their retreating general.

A woman named Jael, the wife of Heber, waited for Barak. Jael had given [Sisera] warm milk and then killed him as he slept.

Daily Wisdom for Women

13 MAY

ADONAI, MY LORD

The LORD says to my Lord: "Sit at My right hand until I make Your enemies a footstool for Your feet."

PSALM 110:1

Unless you know that the Hebrew word *Adonai* refers to God alone, it's easy to misinterpret this passage. It's obvious that David understands the mystery of the Trinity and calls his Messiah "God, Adonai," recognizing his Savior's equality with God the Father. This one passage represents two of the personalities within the Godhead.

One-Minute Meditations

14 MAY

Finding the Messiah

*He found first his own brother Simon and said to him,
"We have found the Messiah."*

JOHN 1:41

Andrew, speaking in today's scripture, found the Messiah and couldn't wait to tell his brother, Simon. That's how we all feel when God's light is at last turned on inside the dungeons of our souls. How blessed for Andrew that his brother responded, and they shared the love of the Lord together.

Daily Wisdom for Women

15 MAY

The Stone the Builders Rejected

The stone which the builders rejected has become the chief corner stone.

Psalm 118:22

When a building is started, a cornerstone must be placed precisely, because the rest of the structure is lined up with it. Likewise, Jesus Christ is the cornerstone of the Church. And His Church is dependent upon Him for guidance. Is Jesus Christ the true cornerstone of your church? If you're looking for a church home, make sure you check the "foundation" first.

One-Minute Meditations

16 MAY

God's Protection for Widows

The Lord. . .will establish the boundary of the widow.

PROVERBS 15:25

Just after the last [Christmas] gift had been purchased, a severe heart attack overtook my dad.

My mother's first concern was how she might continue caring for her children. Mom donned a beret and smock and began selling pastel portraits. No matter what her hardships, Mom has honored God, in whom she placed her faith and the care of her life.

Daily Wisdom for Women

17 MAY

An Angel Visits Gideon

The angel of the Lord appeared to him and said to him, "The Lord is with you, O valiant warrior."

JUDGES 6:12

Have you ever felt that the weight of the world rested on your shoulders? Well, that's Gideon for you. The Lord answered Gideon with the same resounding message of assurance which He always gives to His servants: "Surely I will be with you" (Judges 6:16). God is with us in the fight.

One-Minute Meditations

18 MAY

Mary Requests Christ's Help

When the wine ran out, the mother of Jesus said to Him, "They have no wine."

JOHN 2:3

Jesus was not yet ready to declare publicly to Israel His true identity. And performing an astonishing miracle would undoubtedly draw unwanted attention to Him. Yet how could Christ possibly deny his mother the favor she asked? Confident of His intervention, Mary admonishes the servants, "Whatever He says to you, do it" (John 2:5).

Daily Wisdom for Women

19 MAY

Knowing God's Precepts

*Teach me Your statutes.
Make me understand the way of Your precepts.*

Psalm 119:26–27

Have you ever felt as if you've reached the end of the road and the only choice ahead of you is a brick wall? When you reach that point the only remedy is to look up! God is waiting for you to come to your senses. Understand and walk in the way of His precepts by meditating on God's Word.

One-Minute Meditations

20 MAY

Seek Wisdom, Not Self

*When a wicked man comes, contempt also comes,
and with dishonor comes scorn.*

PROVERBS 18:3

Women become vulnerable the instant truth is replaced with desire. So how can we teach our daughters to be wise? By acquiring knowledge ourselves. As we study God's Word in times of peace, our first thoughts during periods of crisis will be scripture. If we just do what God expects of us, we gain strength of character.

Daily Wisdom for Women

21 MAY

A Great Teacher

"Truly, truly, I say to you, unless one is born again he cannot see the kingdom of God."

JOHN 3:3

Nicodemus came to Christ by night. Although the Pharisees had reached the conclusion that Christ was sent from God, they hadn't bridged the gap to full understanding. Nicodemus obviously heard what Christ said and couldn't shake it loose from his thoughts. He sought the truth, so Christ made it as clear as a starlit night.

One-Minute Meditations

22 MAY

Strength Is Not in Numbers

The LORD said to Gideon, "The people who are with you are too many for Me to give Midian into their hands, for Israel would become boastful, saying, 'My own power has delivered me.'"

JUDGES 7:2

Gideon's "battle strategy" included amassing a multitude which would obliterate the Midianites. God told him no. Instead, God had Gideon keep whittling down that number of troops. Finally, with three hundred men, Gideon crossed the Jordan and won the battle.

Daily Wisdom for Women

23 MAY

Fearfully and Wonderfully Made

For You formed my inward parts; You wove me in my mother's womb. I will give thanks to You, for I am fearfully and wonderfully made.

Psalm 139:13–14

Each of us has not only an inborn sense that there is a God, but also an understanding that we possess a designed intent. Had He not willed your very existence, you would not have happened. God wants to use your life to further His kingdom.

One-Minute Meditations

24 MAY

The Virtuous Woman

An excellent wife, who can find?... The heart of her husband trusts in her.... She does him good and not evil all the days of her life.

PROVERBS 31:10–12

The virtuous woman in today's scripture did good to her husband and not evil. All her activities were geared toward building up her home. Through lonely hours, this is the example I followed. When my husband finally graduated with a degree, his family remained intact.

Daily Wisdom for Women

25 MAY

Absolute Assurance of Eternal Life

"He who believes in the Son has eternal life."

JOHN 3:36

Rigo Lopez turned on the TV. Billy Graham's voice carried to him a message of hope. "You can have absolute assurance today of your salvation." Those words became like a heat-seeking missile, going directly to the source of pain in Rigo's heart. God's Word says we can have absolute assurance of eternal life. Rigo grasped onto God's truth and his life was transformed.

One-Minute Meditations

26 MAY

An Arrogant King

*"Speak now, in the hearing of all the leaders of Shechem,
'Which is better for you, that. . .all the sons of Jerubbaal,
rule over you, or that one man rule over you?' "*

Judges 9:2

After the death of Jerubbaal, his own son devised a plot to become king. "Then God sent an evil spirit between Abimelech and the men of Shechem" (Judges 9:23). God always intervenes to bring the course of history in line with His design.

Daily Wisdom for Women

27 MAY

Praise and Dance

*Let everything that has breath praise the Lord.
Praise the Lord!*

Psalm 150:6

True worship is using our entire beings to give Him the glory He deserves. Whom are we to praise? The Lord! Where are we to praise? Wherever His congregation gathers. For what are we praising? For who He is, what He's done, and the way He's done it. How are we to praise? With our voices, our instruments, and our bodies.

One-Minute Meditations

MAY 28

ENCOUNTER AT THE WELL

*There came a woman of Samaria to draw water.
Jesus said to her, "Give Me a drink."*

JOHN 4:7

Shocked, the woman responded, "How is it that You, being a Jew, ask me for a drink since I am a Samaritan woman?" (John 4:9). Jesus Christ goes right to the heart of her problem. And when she asked where to get this living water, He explained the process of eternal life to her.

Daily Wisdom for Women

29 MAY

A Hasty Vow

Now Jephthah the Gileadite was a valiant warrior.

JUDGES 11:1

The Israelites once again began to serve Baal. Finally, the Israelites acknowledged their sin, and God chose Jephthah as their judge. Victorious over many enemies, Jephthah made a vow that he would sacrifice to God of whatever came out of his house first. Tragically, Jephthah's only child, a daughter, bounded out the front door to meet him. She was sacrificed, just as Jephthah had promised.

One-Minute Meditations

30 MAY

All Is Vanity!

*"Vanity of vanities," says the Preacher,
"Vanity of vanities! All is vanity."*

ECCLESIASTES 1:2

At the end of his life, King Solomon concludes that the things of earth are but fleeting. Perhaps you, too, are prone to reflect on the tasks which occupy your days, concluding that nothing gets accomplished. As we go through Ecclesiastes, [we see that] Solomon had experienced the best the world has to offer. . .and it wasn't enough.

Daily Wisdom for Women

31 MAY

HEALED MIRACULOUSLY

For an angel of the Lord went down at certain seasons into the pool and stirred up the water; whoever then first, after the stirring up of the water, stepped in was made well.

JOHN 5:4

Do you wish to get well? Do you honestly desire to rid yourself of the things which debilitate? True healing of our souls requires a change of direction. Only God knows the content of one's heart.

One-Minute Meditations

1 JUNE

Unremarkable Lives

*Now Ibzan. . .judged Israel seven years.
Then Ibzan died and was buried in Bethlehem.*

JUDGES 12:8–10

How can we discern the will of God for our lives? Daily prayer is definitely the main source. This involves not only relating our needs to God, but also listening for His directions. For He never meant for us to traverse through this maze called life without the road maps He would supply.

Daily Wisdom for Women

2 JUNE

Search for Happiness

*I said to myself, "Come now, I will test you with pleasure.
So enjoy yourself." And behold, it too was futility.*

Ecclesiastes 2:1

Remember when you thought that new dress or outfit would bring you happiness? And it did until you wore it again and again. Then you moved on to bigger things. All that his eyes desired he achieved, but it finally occurred to Solomon that in the end he would die and leave it all.

One-Minute Meditations

3 JUNE

Jesus, Bread of Life

"This is the bread which came down out of heaven; not as the fathers ate and died; he who eats this bread will live forever."

JOHN 6:58

To truly partake of Christ is to accept Him as He is, fully God and fully man, sent from God, recognizing our need for Him. He came first to the Jews, but they refused the message. What is your response?

Daily Wisdom for Women

4 JUNE

SAMSON IS CONCEIVED

"Behold now, you are barren and have borne no children, but you shall conceive and give birth to a son."

JUDGES 13:3

God made it clear that from the moment of conception this was, in fact, a son. Abortion advocates tell us otherwise, despite the Lord's pronouncement that following the union of the sperm and egg, a unique human has been created. Truly the wisdom of the Lord defies time, technology, and human arrogance.

One-Minute Meditations

5 JUNE

A Case against Abortion

*Just as you do not know the path of the wind and
how bones are formed in the womb of the pregnant woman,
so you do not know the activity of God who makes all things.*

ECCLESIASTES 11:5

As women, it's up to us to uphold the sanctity of life. Each life comes into this world with a purpose. Abortion is wrong, no matter what. Exercising our option to go against [God's] commandments is never the right choice.

Daily Wisdom for Women

6 JUNE

Not Even His Brothers Believed

For not even His brothers were believing in Him.

JOHN 7:5

One of the most difficult challenges any believer faces is reaching her family with Christ's message. Although Jesus' own brothers had daily viewed His sinless life, they were blind to who He really was. Their unbelief had been prophesied in Psalm 69:8: "I have become estranged from my brothers." Christ's half brothers were completely in tune with the world, and not with God.

One-Minute Meditations

7 JUNE

Samson Grows Older, Not Wiser

Then the woman gave birth to a son and named him Samson.

JUDGES 13:24

As Samson struck out on his own, the first thing he did was fall in love with a Philistine woman. Later, Samson set torches between pairs of three hundred foxes and turned them loose to burn the Philistines' grain supply. Samson's misuse of power caused the Philistines to kill his bride and her father. Samson clearly was not in the Lord's will.

Daily Wisdom for Women

8 JUNE

A Time to Mourn

There is an appointed time for everything...a time to weep and a time to laugh; a time to mourn and a time to dance.

ECCLESIASTES 3:1, 4

Occasionally a time of mourning enters our lives, sometimes stealing in almost silently, sometimes brashly breaking down the door to our sense of security. Neither path reflects nor distorts the fact that God loves us. But tragedy and mourning are both part of the "rhythm of life."

One-Minute Meditations

9 JUNE

AN ADULTEROUS WOMAN

"Teacher, this woman has been caught in adultery, in the very act. Now in the Law Moses commanded us to stone such women; what then do You say?"

JOHN 8:4–5

The Pharisees meant to pit Christ's ruling against what Moses had commanded. However, their plot backfired! Then, "He straightened up, and said to them, 'He who is without sin among you, let him be the first to throw a stone at her.' " (John 8:7).

Daily Wisdom for Women

10 JUNE

SAMSON USES BRAWN, NOT BRAINS

*After this it came about that he loved a woman
in the valley of Sorek, whose name was Delilah.*

JUDGES 16:4

The rest of the story is the stuff of legend as the Philistines use Delilah to bring down Samson. "She. . .called for a man and had him shave off. . .his hair" (Judges 16:19).

But Samson's hair grew back. In the assembly hall where the Philistines gathered, Samson brought down the house, killing himself and three thousand Philistines.

One-Minute Meditations

11 JUNE

THE DAYS OF YOUR YOUTH

Remember also your Creator in the days of your youth, before the evil days come and the years draw near when you will say, "I have no delight in them."

ECCLESIASTES 12:1

The Book of Ecclesiastes concludes with the admonition not only to remember our Creator when we are young, but to continue following His precepts throughout our time on earth. Have you forgotten the God of your youth? It's not too late to turn it all around.

Daily Wisdom for Women

12 JUNE

JESUS, LIGHT OF THE WORLD

As He passed by, He saw a man blind from birth.

JOHN 9:1

When you walk into a darkened room, you reach for the light switch. However, the man in today's scripture had been born blind.

But Jesus intervened. "He spat on the ground, and made clay of the spittle, and applied the clay to his eyes, and said to him, 'Go, wash in the pool of Siloam,' (which is translated, Sent). So he went away and washed, and came back seeing" (John 9:6–7).

One-Minute Meditations

13 JUNE

Ruth, Faithful Daughter-in-Law

They took for themselves Moabite women as wives; the name of the one was Orpah and the name of the other Ruth.

RUTH 1:4

Ruth was a young woman when her husband died. However, God had a glorious plan. In time, Ruth would become Boaz's bride and mother to his son, a son whose lineage would include David and the Messiah, Jesus Christ.

Daily Wisdom for Women

14 JUNE

Hannah's Prayer Is Observed

She, greatly distressed, prayed to the Lord and wept bitterly.

1 Samuel 1:10

Hannah has gone to the temple year after year and pleaded with God for a son. Finally, Eli gave Hannah a blessing, "Go in peace; and may the God of Israel grant your petition that you have asked of Him" (1 Samuel 1:17). The persistent prayers of a Christian woman should never be underestimated!

One-Minute Meditations

15 JUNE

The Song of Solomon

"Arise, my darling, my beautiful one, and come along!"
SONG OF SOLOMON 2:13

Approaching this book with the understanding that it's a love story enables the reader to appreciate its lyrical quality. [It] also addresses issues of pertinence to women. Understanding ourselves and our mates, the importance of intimacy and purity, and the concept of fidelity within the marital union are discussed. Most importantly, the Song of Solomon explores the spiritual relationship we have with God.

Daily Wisdom for Women

**16
JUNE**

JESUS, THE GOOD SHEPHERD

*"The sheep hear his voice, and he calls
his own sheep by name and leads them out."*

JOHN 10:3

Sheep need constant overseeing and strict boundaries. The shepherd is the ultimate caregiver!

God calls us by name, just as the shepherd has pet names for his sheep. Someday, when our Good Shepherd calls us home to heaven, we'll hear the name He calls us.

One-Minute Meditations

17 JUNE

Samuel Is Born

It came about in due time, after Hannah had conceived, that she gave birth to a son; and she named him Samuel, saying, "Because I have asked him of the Lord."

1 Samuel 1:20

Hannah wanted to keep her promise to God. After Samuel was born and she had weaned him, she took him to the temple. She said to Eli, "For this boy I prayed. . . . So I have also dedicated him to the Lord" (1 Samuel 1:27–28).

Daily Wisdom for Women

18 JUNE

Isaiah, a Major Prophet

*Listen. . .for the L*ORD *speaks,
"Sons I have reared and brought up, but they have revolted
against Me. . . . My people do not understand."*

Isaiah 1:2–3

Reading Isaiah provides a necessary heart check. Like Israel, if we fail to turn from our defiant ways, we must ask, "Where will you be stricken again, as you continue in your rebellion? The whole head is sick and the whole heart is faint" (Isaiah 1:5).

One-Minute Meditations

19 JUNE

Jesus Raises Lazarus

*Now a certain man was sick, Lazarus of Bethany. . . .
Therefore the sisters sent to Him, saying,
"Lord, behold, he whom You love is sick."*

JOHN 11:1, 3 NKJV

It took all the human restraint He possessed not to run to Lazarus's aid. But Jesus had a greater purpose. At the tomb Jesus called: "Lazarus, come forth" (John 11:43 NKJV). And Lazarus walked out. Have you allowed Christ to exercise His authority to bring you forth to new life?

Daily Wisdom for Women

Hannah Acknowledges Her Savior

*Then Hannah prayed and said,
"My heart exults in the LORD.... I rejoice in Your salvation."*

1 Samuel 2:1

Hannah is very aware of the one truth of her life and she expresses it eloquently: "I rejoice in Your salvation." She took to heart all that God had done for her people in the past and accepted that He alone could change her circumstances. To whom do you turn for solutions?

One-Minute Meditations

21 JUNE

Listen, My Children

Hear the word of the LORD....
Give ear to the instruction of our God.

ISAIAH 1:10

The prophet Isaiah was sent to warn the people of impending disaster. Here he uses an example from the past, that of Sodom and Gomorrah, to point to their own imminent doom if they fail to listen. "Hear the word of the Lord," he reminds them. But they refused to obey. "Everyone did what was right in his own eyes" (Judges 21:25).

Daily Wisdom for Women

22 JUNE

Mary's Expensive Gift

Mary then took a pound of very costly perfume of pure nard, and anointed the feet of Jesus.

JOHN 12:3

The gift which Mary used to anoint Jesus' feet was extravagant, costing a year's wages. Mary's lavish use of this burial perfume represented her deep gratitude to Christ, but the disciples called the gift "a waste" (Matthew 26:8–9; John 12:4–6). [They] had missed what He had been relating to them concerning His own death.

One-Minute Meditations

23 JUNE

A Man of God Speaks to Eli

*"Did I not choose them from all the tribes of Israel to be My priests?...
Why do you kick at My sacrifice?"*

1 Samuel 2:28–29

When God's leaders fail to follow obediently, they are removed from their positions. Eli and his family had been chosen by the Lord to be priests in the temple. Yet Eli and his sons had misused their authority. And there's no way the Lord could allow them to continue to be priests in the temple.

Daily Wisdom for Women

24 JUNE

THE WORK OF THEIR HANDS

For You have abandoned Your people, the house of Jacob, because they are filled with influences from the east.

ISAIAH 2:6

Let's compare the things which distracted Israel from worship with our own possible list. First, they were "filled with influences from the east." Next, "their land has also been filled with silver and gold" (Isaiah 2:7). They had methods of travel in abundance. And, last but not least, their land was filled with idols.

One-Minute Meditations

25 JUNE

His Light Dispels Darkness

*"I have come as Light into the world,
so that everyone who believes in Me will not remain in darkness."*

JOHN 12:46

If you have a question about one verse of scripture, first pray that God's Spirit will provide enlightenment. Then, get a good study Bible that has cross-referencing indexed along with the text. With such a guide at hand, God's Word becomes clearer and your faith is sure to deepen.

Daily Wisdom for Women

26 JUNE

Learning to Hear God's Voice

The LORD called Samuel; and he said, "Here I am."

1 Samuel 3:4

"Speak, LORD, for Your servant is listening " (1 Samuel 3:9). The Lord proceeded to say to Samuel, "Behold. . .I will carry out against Eli all that I have spoken concerning his house, from beginning to end" (1 Samuel 3:11–12). This rattled Samuel's sense of well-being. Samuel wanted to keep this from Eli, but Eli asked for the truth, and Samuel related the message as God presented it.

One-Minute Meditations

27 JUNE

The Lord Provides a Sign

"Behold, a virgin will be with child and bear a son, and she will call His name Immanuel."

Isaiah 7:14

God said that He would provide a sign of the coming Messiah. This prediction of Christ's conception was delivered over seven hundred years before He was actually born. In announcing to Joseph that Mary was with child by the power of God's Spirit, the angel used these exact words from Isaiah.

Daily Wisdom for Women

28 JUNE

Jesus' Last Passover

He girded Himself. Then He poured water into the basin, and began to wash the disciples' feet and to wipe them with the towel with which He was girded.

John 13:4–5

How difficult it must have been for Christ to say good-bye to them, knowing they still didn't fully comprehend His impending death! So Jesus set about to love them. By His example, He wanted to show them that they were called to be servants.

One-Minute Meditations

29 JUNE

THE DAY OF THE LORD

*Wail, for the day of the LORD is near!
It will come as destruction from the Almighty.*

ISAIAH 13:6

Isaiah's words are filled with prophecy concerning the impending destruction of the Babylonian Empire. It may be difficult to separate which things are happening in Isaiah's day and which are reserved for the day of the Lord. For there is a specific time in history when the final judgment against the disobedient will take place.

Daily Wisdom for Women

30 JUNE

WHERE GOD EXISTS

"In My Father's house are many dwelling places."

JOHN 14:2

Jesus Christ has promised to prepare a place for us in heaven. Does it get any better than that? The only problem is that we have to wait down here until He's got our mansion ready for us. There are days when it's so hard to stay tied to earth, especially with the realization that a perfect place exists.

Heaven is truly the place where God exists.

One-Minute Meditations

1 JULY

The Ark of the Covenant

And the ark of God was taken.

1 Samuel 4:11

The sacred ark of the covenant was captured.

As long as the Israelites kept the ark with them, the Lord's presence was among them. However, their defeat had taken place long before the ark had been captured. The Israelites had forsaken the true God, and He was about to teach them what life would be like without Him on their side.

Daily Wisdom for Women

2 JULY

SAMUEL'S WICKED SONS

His sons, however, did not walk in his ways.

1 SAMUEL 8:3

Unlike Eli, Samuel had walked in obedience to God. His children chose not to follow in his footsteps of faith. "Then all the elders of Israel gathered together and came to Samuel at Ramah; and they said to him, 'Behold, you have grown old, and your sons do not walk in your ways. Now appoint a king for us' " (1 Samuel 8:4–5).

One-Minute Meditations

3 JULY

Jesus, the True Vine

"I am the vine, you are the branches; he who abides in Me and I in him, he bears much fruit, for apart from Me you can do nothing."

JOHN 15:5

Christ used word pictures to clarify concepts to His followers. And the images in this parable were extremely familiar to them.

This offer to abide in the vine is extended to all who hear the gospel message. Have you responded? And how diligently are you abiding?

Daily Wisdom for Women

4 JULY

DEPENDENCE DAY

"Then the glory of the Lord will be revealed."

Isaiah 40:5

Only when we are totally dependent on our Redeemer are we are truly free!

Carefully woven throughout chapters forty to sixty-six of Isaiah are specific portraits of Christ, presented by the names He called Himself, like a shepherd.

Then we see Him as the Counselor. We can know Him as Creator. Jesus is the First and the Last.

One-Minute Meditations

5 JULY

A New Name for Israel

*The nations will see your righteousness. . . .
And you will be called by a new name.*

ISAIAH 62:2

Whenever God sets about to perform a work of regeneration, He also provides a new name.

In today's scripture the Lord is addressing His people's repeated disobedience which has caused Israel's name to became synonymous with "Forsaken" and "Desolate" (Isaiah 62:4). However, they will one day become the "Redeemed" of the Lord.

Daily Wisdom for Women

6 JULY

THE ROLE OF THE HOLY SPIRIT

"And He, when He comes, will convict the world concerning sin and righteousness and judgment."

JOHN 16:8

The disciples had to know that God's Spirit, which in the past had come upon men and women for equipping, now dwelled inside them. The Holy Spirit would be with them to guide and convict the world concerning sin, righteousness, and judgment. Are you aware of these things in your own life?

One-Minute Meditations

7 JULY

SAUL, ISRAEL'S KING

*He had a son whose name was Saul,
a choice and handsome man, and there was not a more
handsome person than he among the sons of Israel.*

1 SAMUEL 9:2

Isn't that exactly what our society looks for in the way of leaders? But outward appearance means nothing if that person isn't fully committed to God.

God chose Saul to be Israel's king so that [they] might eventually learn their need for spiritual discernment.

Daily Wisdom for Women

8 JULY

Heaven...His Throne, Earth...His Footstool

"Heaven is My throne and the earth is My footstool. Where then is a house you could build for Me?"

Isaiah 66:1

The temple was the earthly place that God established for worship, so that men and women could fellowship together in praise of their Creator. However, true worship begins in our hearts. Jesus Christ is not only our Creator, but He is head of the Church and the world is His footstool.

One-Minute Meditations

9 JULY

An Intimate Conversation

> *"I glorified You on the earth, having accomplished the work which You have given Me to do."*

JOHN 17:4

We are privileged to overhear Jesus as He speaks to the Father.

Christ's prayer to the Father also includes concern for those whom the Father has given to Him. Then Jesus also asks the Father to keep us in His name. Christ prayed that God's power would keep us from being swayed by the world.

Daily Wisdom for Women

10 JULY

CALLED TO CONQUER?

"You shall anoint him to be prince over My people Israel; and he will deliver My people from the hand of the Philistines."

1 SAMUEL 9:16

Notice that Saul's call was to conquer the Philistines. His anointing had been done secretly, but now Samuel assembled all Israel. When Saul failed to appear, "They inquired further of the LORD. . . . So the LORD said, 'Behold, he is hiding himself by the baggage'" (1 Samuel 10:22).

One-Minute Meditations

11 JULY

Jeremiah's Revival

*"Before I formed you in the womb. . .I consecrated you;
I have appointed you a prophet to the nations."*

JEREMIAH 1:5

Knowing that he was consecrated should have given Jeremiah confidence. However, like any true prophet, he felt consumed because of his own inadequacies. "But the LORD said. . .'I have put My words in your mouth'" (Jeremiah 1:7, 9). And Jeremiah proceeded forward, fulfilling his mission.

Daily Wisdom for Women

12 JULY

JESUS IS ARRESTED AND TRIED

Now Judas also, who was betraying Him, knew the place, for Jesus had often met there with His disciples.

JOHN 18:2

Judas's scheme was calculated and well-planned. When the capture was imminent, Judas handed Jesus over to the authorities for thirty pieces of silver. Did membership in this treacherous mob impart courage to Judas? We only know that later he would completely despair of his action and commit suicide.

One-Minute Meditations

13 JULY

Saul's Reign Ends in Disgrace

"Fill your horn with oil and go; I will send you to Jesse the Bethlehemite, for I have selected a king for Myself among his sons."

1 Samuel 16:1

Poised for battle, Saul grew tired of waiting for Samuel to come and offer a burnt offering to the Lord to ensure the victory. Therefore, Saul offered it himself. He had usurped the God-given role of Samuel.

So in today's scripture we read that the Lord chose another king.

Daily Wisdom for Women

14 JULY

Jeremiah's Vision

"I will pronounce My judgments on them concerning all their wickedness, whereby they have forsaken Me."

Jeremiah 1:16

Despite all God's warnings, the people failed to respond to Him unless they were in dire pain. Therefore, the Lord encourages Jeremiah by saying, "Do not be dismayed. . . for I am with you to deliver you" (Jeremiah 1:17, 19).

We humans are resilient as long as we know we're not abandoned. God always provides a way through.

One-Minute Meditations

15 JULY

QUESTION THE WITNESSES

*"Why do you question Me?
Question those who have heard what I spoke to them;
they know what I said."*

JOHN 18:21

As we go out into a world that is hostile to the gospel message, there are those who listen to our testimony and then draw near to its refreshing waters. Others vow that nothing will force them to make a life change. And there are those whose hearts are closed to receiving the truth.

Daily Wisdom for Women

16 JULY

DAVID SLINGS A STONE

*"Who is this uncircumcised Philistine,
that he should taunt the armies of the living God?"*

1 SAMUEL 17:26

David, while still a youth, came up against a giant man. This superhuman had the audacity to taunt Israel's God. And David refused to allow this attitude to stand unchallenged.

Then David said, "I come to you in the name of the LORD of hosts, the God of the armies of Israel, whom you have taunted. This day the LORD will deliver you up into my hands" (1 Samuel 17:45–46).

One-Minute Meditations

17 JULY

A Promise of Unity

*"In those days the house of Judah
will walk with the house of Israel."*

JEREMIAH 3:18

Jeremiah delivered hope to the people of Israel.

This prophecy related God's future plans for Israel. First, the ark of the covenant would be gone. Jerusalem would be where all nations would gather in the name of the Lord. The houses of Judah and Israel would once again be united. True peace will reign in Israel when Christ returns.

Daily Wisdom for Women

18 JULY

A Sign on the Cross

Pilate answered, "What I have written I have written."
JOHN 19:22

God overruled the Jews' request when Pilate refused to change what had been written. Pilate knew Christ was exactly who He claimed to be, King of the Jews, the promised Messiah.

Pilate had to live in this place long after Christ was gone. Pilate had already stated, "I find no guilt in Him" (John 19:6). Yet Pilate lacked the gumption to stand by his strong conviction.

One-Minute Meditations

19 JULY

The Lord's Anointed

"I will not stretch out my hand against. . .the Lord's anointed."

1 Samuel 24:10

Saul's rejection by God fueled his anger, causing his vengeful spirit to pursue David relentlessly.

David came upon Saul as he slept. And David's followers suggested that he kill Saul. However, David settled for cutting off a corner of Saul's robe as a gesture of his respect for God's anointed.

Despite his circumstances, David would allow the Lord charge over this matter.

Daily Wisdom for Women

20 JULY

Christ as Mediator

"Their Redeemer is strong, the Lord of hosts is His name."

Jeremiah 50:34

Who is this Redeemer? "For there is one God, and one mediator also between God and men, the man Christ Jesus" (1 Timothy 2:5–6).

Abraham looked forward in time to redemption by the Messiah, while we take a view back in time to the cross on which our Redeemer died. Christ then becomes the central focus, for both the Old and New Testaments.

One-Minute Meditations

21 JULY

Crown of Mockery

Pilate then took Jesus and scourged Him. And the soldiers twisted together a crown of thorns and put it on His head.

John 19:1–2

They pretended to shower Him with all the outward trappings of royalty. But this homage was one of cruel mockery.

"He was despised and forsaken of men, a man of sorrows and acquainted with grief" (Isaiah 53:3).

Daily Wisdom for Women

22 JULY

Jonathan, Faithful to the End

The Philistines overtook Saul and his sons; and the Philistines killed Jonathan.

1 SAMUEL 31:2

Jonathan walked a tightrope, remaining faithful to God, to Saul, and to David. Considering Saul's obsession with killing David, this task took on monstrous proportions.

Jonathan's time was spent trying to help David keep one step ahead of Saul. Are you a faithful, loving, and unforgettable friend?

One-Minute Meditations

23 JULY

His Glory Has Departed

The Lord has become like an enemy.
He has swallowed up Israel.

Lamentations 2:5

The book of Lamentations was read annually by the Jews as a reminder of the fall of Jerusalem and the destruction of the temple. The words were meant to remind Israel of all they'd lost as a result of their refusal to worship the true God.

Daily Wisdom for Women

24 JULY

THE FIRST TO VIEW THE RESURRECTION

"They have taken away the Lord out of the tomb, and we do not know where they have laid Him."

JOHN 20:2

"She turned around, and saw Jesus standing there, and did not know that it was Jesus" (John 20:14).

But then He said, "Mary!" And the sound of His voice calmed her frantic fears, dried her tears, and warmed her heart.

One-Minute Meditations

25 JULY

David Learns of Saul's Death

"And Saul and Jonathan his son are dead also."

2 Samuel 1:4

A young Amalekite man had related to David that Saul and Jonathan were dead. Then he confessed that Saul had begged him to kill him.

First David led Israel in a time of mourning for Saul. Following this expression of sorrow came a time of retribution. What an example David was, as he refused to gloat over Saul's death.

Daily Wisdom for Women

26 JULY

Ezekiel's Call

While I was by the river Chebar among the exiles, the heavens were opened and I saw visions of God.

Ezekiel 1:1

Ezekiel's life plan became forever altered when he was taken in Nebuchadnezzar's second siege against Jerusalem. Never again would he view the temple. However, the Lord gave him a vision of a new temple and another Jerusalem. His call was to prophesy concerning Judah and Jerusalem, Israel's coming restoration, and the temple.

One-Minute Meditations

27 JULY

Jesus Holds a Fish Fry

But when the day was now breaking, Jesus stood on the beach; yet the disciples did not know that it was Jesus.

John 21:4

It was shortly after the Resurrection.

Here Christ renewed His leadership invitation to Peter. When Peter requested information concerning the future of the disciple John, Jesus replied, "If I want him to remain until I come, what is that to you? You follow Me!" (John 21:22)

Daily Wisdom for Women

28 JULY

David, King of Judah

Then the men of Judah came and there anointed David king over the house of Judah.

2 Samuel 2:4

We assume that once God makes His choice in a leader that everyone else then follows that person. Nothing could be further from the truth. Ishbosheth ruled in Gilead for two years, while the house of Judah followed David.

"David became greater and greater, for the Lord God of hosts was with him" (2 Samuel 5:10).

One-Minute Meditations

29 JULY

Ezekiel Speaks to the Lost

"Son of man, go to the house of Israel and speak with My words to them."

EZEKIEL 3:4

How did you become a Christian? By hearing the Word of God? The powerful Word of God convicts our hearts of sin and turns us toward the Lord.

At times we are unwilling to risk presenting the gospel message because of personal rejection. However, the outcome isn't our problem, it's God's.

Daily Wisdom for Women

30 JULY

CHRIST ASCENDS INTO HEAVEN

"John baptized with water, but you will be baptized with the Holy Spirit not many days from now."

ACTS 1:5

The disciples had learned how to live the Christian life from observing Jesus during His three years of ministry. Now they would watch Christ ascend to heaven; no longer would they speak to Him face-to-face. However, Jesus sent them His Spirit, that they might have God's power within them as His Church began.

One-Minute Meditations

31 JULY

The Desire of David

*"Go, do all that is in your mind,
for the Lord is with you."*

2 SAMUEL 7:3

How can we truly discern the will of God? My own decision-making process is threefold. First, I pray, seeking God's wisdom concerning the issue. Next, I read His Word, making sure that what is in my heart isn't in conflict with His clear messages. And last, I look for confirming circumstances. When all three of these steps fall in line, I can be fairly certain that I am acting in obedience to God's will.

Daily Wisdom for Women

1 AUGUST

The Same Vision

*Then the Spirit lifted me up,
and I heard a great rumbling sound behind me.*

Ezekiel 3:12

Ezekiel's vision can be compared to one that John had.

John records, "After these things I looked, and behold, a door standing open in heaven, and the first voice which I had heard, like the sound of a trumpet speaking with me, said, 'Come up here, and I will show you what must take place after these things' " (Revelation 4:1).

One-Minute Meditations

2 AUGUST

The Day of Pentecost

When the day of Pentecost had come...
they were all filled with the Holy Spirit.

Acts 2:1, 4

Pentecost was not new to the Jews. But now Christ poured out His Spirit on those who believed in Him, fulfilling the promise and prophecy of Joel. "I will pour out My Spirit in those days" (Joel 2:29).

Daily Wisdom for Women

3 AUGUST

DAVID

Now when evening came David arose from his bed and walked around on the roof of the king's house, and from the roof he saw a woman bathing.

2 SAMUEL 11:2

The Bible presents the true account of man's record on this earth, warts and all! David should have accompanied his men into battle. David succumbed to temptation. David tried to cover his tracks.

David then had Uriah sent to the front lines, where he was killed.

One-Minute Meditations

4 AUGUST

Always a Remnant

*"Therefore I will also withdraw,
and My eye will have no pity and I will not spare."*

Ezekiel 5:11

God is executing judgment on [Israel] because they abandoned their worship of the true God, choosing instead to adopt the ways of the pagan nations which surrounded them.

Many terrible plagues and judgments will take place upon the earth. However, God will bring this remnant of Israel safely through it all.

Daily Wisdom for Women

**5
AUGUST**

At God's Right Hand

*"Therefore having been exalted to the right hand of God,
and having received from the Father the promise of the Holy Spirit,
He has poured forth this which you both see and hear."*

Acts 2:33

Jesus Christ, the fulfillment of all that had been prophesied concerning Israel's Redeemer, had become the bridge between the Old Testament and New Testament. Everything in their history had pointed to this moment.

One-Minute Meditations

6 AUGUST

God Takes David's Child

"Because by this deed you have given occasion to the enemies of the Lord to blaspheme, the child also that is born to you shall surely die."

2 Samuel 12:14

In this particular case, God took the child which David and Bathsheba had conceived in deliberate sin. David had to be held accountable. How could a nation follow him if he failed to obey the God he supposedly served?

Daily Wisdom for Women

7 AUGUST

A False Peace

"So My hand will be against the prophets. . . because they have misled My people by saying, 'Peace!' when there is no peace."

Ezekiel 13:9–10

Just as Ezekiel could not remain complacent in the midst of false peace givers, those of our own day who know the truth are obligated to bring the message of repentance and salvation to others. How else will they hear and respond?

One-Minute Meditations

8 AUGUST

PETER, EMPOWERED AND BOLD

Then Peter, filled with the Holy Spirit, said to them...
"There is no other name under heaven that has been
given among men by which we must be saved."

ACTS 4:8, 12

Peter had become intimidated by the girl who recognized his Galilean accent and accused him of being a follower of Christ.

Now he demonstrates the powerful change which the Holy Spirit has infused into his being.

Daily Wisdom for Women

9 AUGUST

David's Rock, Fortress, and Deliverer

"The Lord is my rock and my fortress and my deliverer."

2 Samuel 22:2

David's understanding of his Lord, using this concept of refuge, is a picture of the peace, comfort, and security we seek for our lives. This analogy was also used to describe the believer's destination of spiritual serenity in the Rock, who is Christ. David depended on the Lord as his rock of faith.

One-Minute Meditations

10 AUGUST

Daniel's Diet

*"Please test your servants for ten days,
and let us be given some vegetables to eat and water to drink."*

DANIEL 1:12

Given to prayer and fasting, two "staples" of his spiritual diet, Daniel convinced the "commander of the officials" (Daniel 1:10) over him to observe the difference between him and those who overindulged at the table of the king.

"Then at the end of the days. . .not one was found like Daniel, Hananiah, Mishael and Azariah" (Daniel 1:18–19).

Daily Wisdom for Women

11 AUGUST

BAPTISM OF REPENTANCE

"Repent, and each of you be baptized in the name of Jesus Christ."
ACTS 2:38

One first has to come face-to-face with her need for salvation. Belief comes in response to presentation of the Word. Also, it's critical to note that the Holy Spirit is given at the moment of repentance (Acts 2:38). In the scripture quoted above, we know for certain that God's timetable for obtaining salvation has begun.

One-Minute Meditations

12 AUGUST

Bathsheba's Influence

"If your sons are careful of their way, to walk before Me in truth with all their heart and with all their soul, you shall not lack a man on the throne of Israel."

1 KINGS 2:4

One of David's sons attempted to use Bathsheba's influence for his personal gain. Adonijah planned a full challenge to Solomon's leadership, even including war. "So King Solomon sent Benaiah the son of Jehoida; and he fell upon him so that he died" (1 Kings 2:25). Adonijah's failure to accept God's plan for the position of king ended in disaster for Adonijah.

Daily Wisdom for Women

13 AUGUST

A Dance in the Fiery Furnace

*"O peoples, nations and men of every language. . .
fall down and worship the golden image that
Nebuchadnezzar the king has set up."*

Daniel 3:4–5

Daniel's friends refused to bow down to any king but the Lord. Therefore, Shadrach, Meshach, and Abednego were bound and then thrown into a fiery furnace.

When the king looked into the furnace he saw a fourth person. Jesus was with Daniel's friends in the fire.

One-Minute Meditations

14 AUGUST

Announced by the Prophets

"But the things which God announced beforehand by the mouth of all the prophets, that His Christ would suffer, He has thus fulfilled. Therefore repent and return, so that your sins may be wiped away."

Acts 3:18–19

Both Jesus and John the Baptist had been killed for preaching the truth about God and the Messiah. Was their message wasted? Not at all. There will always be a remnant who hears and responds.

Daily Wisdom for Women

15 AUGUST

A True Mother's Love

"So give Your servant an understanding heart to judge Your people."

1 Kings 3:9

Two women each were arguing that one infant belonged to her. One of them was lying. "The king said, 'Divide the living child in two, and give half to the one and half to the other' " (1 Kings 3:24–25). Solomon knew that the child's true mother would come to the baby's defense.

Within minutes the issue was resolved, and the real mother held her child again.

One-Minute Meditations

16 AUGUST

Daniel's Deliverance

Then the commissioners and satraps began trying to find a ground of accusation against Daniel in regard to government affairs; but they could find no ground of accusation or evidence of corruption.

Daniel 6:4

Jealousy unchecked renders men and women capable of untold evil. And now that Daniel had been appointed as one of the "commissioners," they plotted against Daniel. They tattled on Daniel. Daniel was then thrust into the lions' den.

Daily Wisdom for Women

17 AUGUST

SAUL AND STEPHEN

Saul was in hearty agreement with putting him to death.
ACTS 8:1

Have you ever committed an action so despicable that you can't imagine God could ever forgive you? After the stoning of Stephen, Saul entered home after home and dragged Christians off to prison.

And then God intervened.

"I am Jesus whom you are persecuting, but get up and enter the city, and it will be told you what you must do" (Acts 9:5–6).

One-Minute Meditations

18 AUGUST

The Whirlwind of Elijah

And it came about when the Lord was about to take up Elijah by a whirlwind to heaven, that Elijah went with Elisha from Gilgal.

2 Kings 2:1

"Elijah said to Elisha, 'Ask what I shall do for you before I am taken from you.' And Elisha said, 'Please, let a double portion of your spirit be upon me'" (2 Kings 2:8–9). Elijah's successor sought confirmation that God's Spirit was with him.

Daily Wisdom for Women

19 AUGUST

Daniel Sees Four Beasts

*Daniel saw a dream and visions in his mind as he lay on his bed. . . .
"And four great beasts were coming up from the sea,
different from one another."*

Daniel 7:1, 3

A nearly identical vision was given to John, who recorded it in the Book of Revelation. This last, terrible beast will be the Antichrist. Do not be deceived by him.

One-Minute Meditations

20 AUGUST

James Is Martyred

*Herod. . .had James the brother of John
put to death with a sword.*

Acts 12:1–2

Perhaps John's own memories now returned to the days when he and his brother James first responded to the Lord's call to follow.

His heart filled with grief for a martyred brother, John contemplated his promise of commitment and then went on with his ministry. The Lord's message and example must have echoed through his mind (Mark 10:40–45).

Daily Wisdom for Women

21 AUGUST

A House Divided Disintegrates

They forsook all the commandments of the LORD....
So the LORD was very angry with Israel.

2 KINGS 17:16, 18

Baal worship was the besetting sin of Israel. Remember that it was for this reason the Lord rejected all the descendants of Israel. What then will happen to our own civilization if we fail to turn the tide of idolatry in which we, too, are steeped?

One-Minute Meditations

**22
AUGUST**

SEVENTY WEEKS HAVE BEEN DECREED

"Seventy weeks have been decreed for your people and your holy city."

DANIEL 9:24

Daniel was the recipient of some of the most critical prophecies concerning the coming Messiah, the Antichrist who would follow, and also the timetable for these events. The kickoff on these hands of time was the decree to restore and rebuild Jerusalem. The Messiah's birth fulfilled Isaiah 7:14. Christ's death fulfilled another part of the prophecy.

Daily Wisdom for Women

23 AUGUST

Aquila and Priscilla, Tentmakers

He stayed with them and they were working, for by trade they were tent-makers.

Acts 18:3

Paul worked as a tentmaker so that he might support his travels within his ministry. Aquila and Priscilla not only assisted him in this task, but they also accompanied Paul on his missionary journey to Syria (Acts 18:18). This married couple also encouraged new believers in teaching "the way of God more accurately" (Acts 18:26).

One-Minute Meditations

24 AUGUST

God Designates the Temple Site

"Give me the site of this threshing floor, that I may build on it an altar to the Lord."

1 CHRONICLES 21:22

King David's disobedience to the Lord brought about a siege of pestilence on the land.

Directly following this incident, God commanded David to obtain this particular property, where Ornan was threshing wheat, for the temple. There stood the altar, the first glimmer of the magnificent temple which would stand on this site.

Daily Wisdom for Women

25 AUGUST

GOOD ANGELS OR BAD ANGELS?

"Do not be afraid, Daniel. . . . I have come in response to your words."
DANIEL 10:12

Have you ever wondered why your prayers seem to take so long to get answered? God had just revealed to Daniel that the Antichrist was going to cause a "complete destruction" in Jerusalem. Consequently, Daniel prayed for three solid weeks before relief finally came. "Then behold, a hand touched me and set me trembling on my hands and knees" (Daniel 10:10).

One-Minute Meditations

26 AUGUST

Paul's Mission in Life

Paul, a bond-servant of Christ Jesus, called as an apostle, set apart for the gospel of God...

ROMANS 1:1

Paul had come to know the true source of life. Remember that this great persecutor of the church had been specifically called by God, who changed not only Paul's life but also his name and priorities.

Daily Wisdom for Women

27 AUGUST

All the King's Horses

Solomon amassed chariots and horsemen.

2 Chronicles 1:14

Solomon's horses were the finest that money could buy. Long before Israel even had a king, the Lord had established certain standards for this monarch. He was not to multiply horses for himself; God didn't want the king's heart to turn away from following Him.

One-Minute Meditations

28 AUGUST

ANTICHRIST, THE RULER TO COME

"In his place a despicable person will arise."

DANIEL 11:21

The Antichrist is a real person who will one day deviously slither onto the scene right on cue. His deception will be so great that people will fail to see his face of evil until "the abomination of desolation" takes place (Matthew 24:15). Jesus Himself warned the Jews about this diabolical person.

Daily Wisdom for Women

29 AUGUST

JUDGE NOT, LEST YE BE JUDGED

But do you suppose this, O man, when you pass judgment on those who practice such things and do the same yourself, that you will escape the judgment of God?

ROMANS 2:3

Those who know little about the Word of God seem to parade about this verse. However, they could not tell you that Paul was addressing hypocrites, those who "know the ordinance of God," and yet practice things which are "worthy of death" (Romans 1:32).

One-Minute Meditations

30 AUGUST

Hezekiah Restores Worship

*Hezekiah became king when he was twenty-five years old. . . .
He did right in the sight of the L*ORD.

2 CHRONICLES 29:1–2

Hezekiah was only twenty-five years old when he became king of Judah.

Instead of following in his father's footsteps, this young king did what was right before the Lord.

During the very first month, worship was reestablished. Hezekiah hearkened to God's voice and his kingdom survived.

Daily Wisdom for Women

31 AUGUST

MICHAEL STANDS GUARD

"Now at that time Michael, the great prince who stands guard over the sons of your people, will arise."

DANIEL 12:1

The prophet Daniel spoke of the archangel Michael because he wanted Israel to be aware that God had already given them a great prince who stands guard over them. Those whose names are written in the book will be spared. God writes the names in His book. It's called the Lamb's Book of Life.

One-Minute Meditations

1 SEPTEMBER

But What about the Jews?

For what does the Scripture say? "Abraham believed God, and it was credited to him as righteousness."

ROMANS 4:3

Salvation is not based on our goodness, but rather on Christ's. For no matter how diligently we try to keep those Ten Commandments, we're going to fail.

God made Abraham, the one the Jews claim as their father, a promise; and he believed God. The reason that Abraham could place his trust in God was because God kept His promises.

Daily Wisdom for Women

2 SEPTEMBER

THE TEMPLE IS REBUILT

"Let him go up to Jerusalem which is in Judah and rebuild the house of the LORD."

EZRA 1:3

Is there a Christmas which really stands out in your memory? Transfer that excitement to how Israel felt when this proclamation finally went out. The Israelites were on the fringe of being brought back to the land God had given them, and their center of worship was about to be restored! Thus, the prophecy recorded in Jeremiah was fulfilled.

One-Minute Meditations

SEPTEMBER 3

Gomer, a Picture of Israel

The Lord said to Hosea, "Go, take to yourself a wife of harlotry and have children of harlotry; for the land commits flagrant harlotry, forsaking the Lord." So he went and took Gomer the daughter of Diblaim, and she conceived and bore him a son.

Hosea 1:2–3

God wanted Israel to understand what it was like to observe the one to whom they were betrothed go off and play the harlot. Hosea reveals the brokenness of God's heart as He watched Israel wander away. Now God was forced to take action against the people He loved in order to bring them back to Him.

Daily Wisdom for Women

4 SEPTEMBER

Peace Despite Our Trials

*Therefore, having been justified by faith,
we have peace with God through our Lord Jesus Christ.*

Romans 5:1

People have scoured every nook and cranny of the globe in search of peace.

Enduring tranquillity cannot be found outside a relationship with Christ. So why can't we just believe it's that simple? Human effort doesn't bring peace. True and lasting peace only comes from Jesus.

One-Minute Meditations

**5
SEPTEMBER**

Construction Is Halted

Then the people of the land discouraged the people of Judah, and frightened them from building.

Ezra 4:4

Can you imagine receiving a loud, clear call from the Lord to take action on your life's work and then have such discouragement? How did the people of Israel keep going? By trusting God instead of rumors, rulers, or rivalry.

Daily Wisdom for Women

6 SEPTEMBER

Yet God Loves Them

*I will love them freely,
for My anger has turned away from them.*

Hosea 14:4

We have sinned. And our holy God is not obligated to forgive us.

We don't deserve a pardon from God; we deserve death. However, He who created us is ready to meet us at the point of repentance and infuse us with such incredible love that we want to love Him back.

One-Minute Meditations

SEPTEMBER 7

SAFETY NET

For the law of the Spirit of life in Christ Jesus has set you free from the law of sin and of death. For what the Law could not do, weak as it was through the flesh, God did.

ROMANS 8:2–3

God's rules provide for us a huge safety net. When we bounce against its sides, we become aware of the need to change our direction.

Daily Wisdom for Women

SEPTEMBER 8

An Evil Plan Backfires

*"The document which you sent to us
has been translated and read before me."*

Ezra 4:17

"Then the work on the house of God in Jerusalem ceased, and it was stopped until the second year of the reign of Darius King of Persia" (Ezra 4:24).

"But the eye of their God was on the elders of the Jews" (Ezra 5:5). When the inquiry was made, it gave the Israelites a chance to expound on how the decree had gone out by Cyrus, king of Babylon, to rebuild the house of God (Ezra 5:6-13).

One-Minute Meditations

9 SEPTEMBER

Joel and a Plague of Locusts

*What the gnawing locust has left, the swarming locust has eaten;...
and what the creeping locust has left, the stripping locust has eaten.*

Joel 1:4

The information contained in the book of Joel is referred to as *eschatology*, or a study of the end times, and parallels other passages in scripture. When Jesus spoke to His disciples, He, too, quoted this prophetic passage, providing additional clarity.

Daily Wisdom for Women

10 SEPTEMBER

Paul's Prayer for the Jews

Brethren, my heart's desire and my prayer to God for them is for their salvation.

ROMANS 10:1

Is the deepest concern of your heart that those whom you love will share heaven with Christ?

Paul presents the simple process by which they can become cleansed of their sins. "If you confess with your mouth Jesus as Lord, and believe in your heart that God raised Him from the dead, you will be saved" (Romans 10:9).

One-Minute Meditations

11 SEPTEMBER

NEHEMIAH AND THE WALLS OF JERUSALEM

*When I heard these words, I sat down and wept and mourned...
and I was fasting and praying before the God of heaven.*

NEHEMIAH 1:4

Although Nehemiah was in Susa, he couldn't forget either his city or its people. So he poured out prayers to the Lord, seeking His wisdom for this renovation project. And God's reply caused him to mourn, fast, and weep, as the solution crystallized: "We have sinned against You; I and my father's house have sinned" (Nehemiah 1:6).

Daily Wisdom for Women

12 SEPTEMBER

Joel Prophesies a Final Judgment

Hasten and come, all you surrounding nations, and gather yourselves there. Bring down, O Lord, Your mighty ones.

Joel 3:11

Jerusalem will be the site of the world's last battle as all the surrounding nations rage against the Holy City. The powerful God of the universe will intervene on Israel's behalf.

At the end of the age, Christ will come back to conquer all those who have attempted to ravage His people and their city.

One-Minute Meditations

SEPTEMBER 13

RENEWING OUR MINDS

Present your bodies a living and holy sacrifice, acceptable to God, which is your spiritual service of worship.

ROMANS 12:1

When an angel came with an announcement that God had asked Mary to bear His son, she knew it would cast a shadow of doubt on her impeccable character. Leaving the results of this decision in the hands of her powerful God, Mary accepted her role as the mother of the Messiah. And during the difficult days which followed, she allowed the Word of God to renew her mind.

Daily Wisdom for Women

14 SEPTEMBER

Relying on God's Strength

*He read from it before the square...
and all the people were attentive to the book of the law.*

NEHEMIAH 8:3

Through inspired teamwork, Nehemiah and the remnant of Israel finished rebuilding the wall in only fifty-two days (Nehemiah 6:15). Even their enemies lost the will to fight, recognizing this accomplishment as coming from the hand of Israel's God.

One-Minute Meditations

15 SEPTEMBER

Amos the Prophet

Thus says the Lord, *"For three transgressions of Damascus and for four I will not revoke its punishment."*

AMOS 1:3

Amos was a simple sheepherder from a small city about ten miles south of Jerusalem. He was called by God to deliver a warning to these stiff-necked, idol-worshipping people of the northern kingdom of Israel: "I am not a prophet. . . . But. . .the Lord said to me, 'Go prophesy to My people Israel' " (Amos 7:14–15).

Daily Wisdom for Women

16 SEPTEMBER

Phoebe, Servant of the Church

*I commend to you our sister Phoebe,
who is a servant of the church which is at Cenchrea...
for she herself has also been a helper of many, and of myself as well.*

ROMANS 16:1–2

Paul viewed dedicated people as living testimonies to all that God's Spirit could accomplish in one's character. Paul deeply appreciated those who walked in step with him to teach and nurture others in order to bring the gospel message to many.

One-Minute Meditations

17 SEPTEMBER

Queen Vashti Spurns the King

*In those days. . .King Ahasuerus. . .
gave a banquet for all his princes and attendants.*

Esther 1:2–3

Can you imagine a party that went on for 187 days? At the same time Queen Vashti had been giving her own banquet. And things were going along quite nicely until. . .

"On the seventh day. . .he commanded. . .to bring Queen Vashti before the king. . .to display her beauty (Esther 1:10–11). Queen Vashti refused to appear on cue.

Daily Wisdom for Women

18 SEPTEMBER

The Apple of God's Eye

"For the day of the Lord draws near on all the nations."

Obadiah 1:15

It was the protection of God that rendered Israel unique as a people. Now their arrogance and lack of true worship rendered them vulnerable to attack. Obadiah calls Israel back to worship their God, but also issues a warning to Edom, the nation intent on wiping them out.

One-Minute Meditations

19 SEPTEMBER

WANTED: SAINTS, DEAD OR ALIVE?

Those who have been sanctified in Christ Jesus, saints by calling, with all who in every place call on the name of our Lord Jesus Christ, their Lord and ours...

1 CORINTHIANS 1:2

As Christians, Christ "will also confirm you to the end, blameless" (1 Corinthians 1:8). This means that because God is faithful, He looks at us and sees the blood of His Son and declares us cleansed from sin.

Daily Wisdom for Women

20 SEPTEMBER

ESTHER IS CHOSEN

*"Let beautiful young virgins be sought for the king. . . .
Then let the young lady who pleases the king be queen in place of Vashti."*

ESTHER 2:2, 4

The book of Esther is a beautiful story of a woman's absolute faith and trust in her God. God placed Esther in a position of authority in order to save the people of Israel.

One-Minute Meditations

21 SEPTEMBER

Jonah Flees God's Call

*But Jonah rose up to flee to Tarshish
from the presence of the Lord.*

Jonah 1:3

Jonah flat out didn't want this job. God always gives men a chance to change, and He set about the task of getting Jonah's attention. First, "there was a great storm. . .

"So the captain approached him and said, '. . .call on your god'" (Jonah 1:4, 6). What a joke! Jonah couldn't pray because he knew exactly who was causing this oceanic disturbance.

Daily Wisdom for Women

22 SEPTEMBER

Hearing God's Spirit Speak

For to us God revealed them through the Spirit;
for the Spirit searches all things, even the depths of God.

1 Corinthians 2:10

Here's an excuse heard often: "We can't try to interpret the Bible ourselves because we'll get confused." But to refuse the Holy Spirit the opportunity to instruct you, as He promised He would, is to refuse true understanding.

One-Minute Meditations

23 SEPTEMBER

Esther Thwarts a Royal Plot

But the plot became known to Mordecai and he told Queen Esther, and Esther informed the king in Mordecai's name.

ESTHER 2:22

Overhearing a private conversation in which a murder plot is discussed, Esther's uncle, Mordecai, a Jew, channeled this information back to his niece, whom the king trusted. Before anyone was aware, God had put a plan into action.

Daily Wisdom for Women

24 SEPTEMBER

Jonah Is Swallowed by a Great Fish

*"Pick me up and throw me into the sea.
Then the sea will become calm for you."*

Jonah 1:12

As soon as they threw Jonah into the water, the sea stopped raging. "And the Lord appointed a great fish to swallow Jonah, and Jonah was in the stomach of the fish three days and three nights" (Jonah 1:17).

Only God has the ability to deliver a great fish to swallow a man whole and not harm him.

One-Minute Meditations

25 SEPTEMBER

OUR BODIES, GOD'S TEMPLE

*Do you not know that you are a temple of God
and that the Spirit of God dwells in you?*

1 CORINTHIANS 3:16

As we go about our business, perhaps it's hard to remember that God indwells us. Paul constantly wrestled with desiring to do the right thing but having his flesh at war with his spirit.

"However, you are not in the flesh but in the Spirit, if indeed the Spirit of God dwells in you" (Romans 8:9–10).

Daily Wisdom for Women

26 SEPTEMBER

Queen Esther Learns of a New Deception

Letters were sent by couriers to all the king's provinces to destroy, to kill and to annihilate all the Jews.

Esther 3:13

And Mordecai replied, "For if you remain silent at this time, relief and deliverance will arise for the Jews from another place and you and your father's house will perish. And who knows whether you have not attained royalty for such a time as this?" (Esther 4:14).

One-Minute Meditations

27 SEPTEMBER

Jonah and God Reach Agreement

"While I was fainting away, I remembered the Lord, and my prayer came to You, into Your holy temple."

Jonah 2:7

There in the belly of the fish, Jonah finally stopped running. Jonah finally pledges allegiance to his God. "But I will sacrifice to You with the voice of thanksgiving. That which I have vowed I will pay. Salvation is from the Lord" (Jonah 2:9). Jonah's ears were finally ready to listen to God.

Daily Wisdom for Women

28 SEPTEMBER

THE NEED FOR GODLY JUDGES

*Or do you not know that the saints will judge the world?
If the world is judged by you, are you not competent
to constitute the smallest law courts?*

1 CORINTHIANS 6:2

God meant for His Church to govern itself. He also intended that the believers work out their differences in love. Today men and women have quit counting on the power of God to rule in their lives and have turned to the "courts of the unbelievers," where they have not found justice.

One-Minute Meditations

29 SEPTEMBER

Queen Esther's Shining Moment

"If I have found favor in the sight of the king. . .may the king and Haman come to the banquet which I will prepare for them, and tomorrow I will do as the king says."

Esther 5:8

At the second banquet she gave, Queen Esther finally related to the king the plot to kill all the Jews, reminding him of his promise to give her anything she desired. Esther was given the wisdom and courage to save her people.

Daily Wisdom for Women

30 SEPTEMBER

Jonah Learns Compassion

When God saw. . .that they turned from their wicked way, then God relented concerning the calamity which He had declared He would bring upon them.

JONAH 3:10

Jonah said he'd risked life and limb for nothing. God acted with compassion, just as Jonah knew He would. And the Ninevites were never punished. "Then the Lord said. . .'Should I not have compassion on Nineveh, the great city in which there are more the 120,000 persons?' " (Jonah 4:10-11).

One-Minute Meditations

1 OCTOBER

To Marry or Stay Single?

*The husband must fulfill his duty to his wife,
and likewise also the wife to her husband.*

1 Corinthians 7:3

If a woman can best serve God as part of a married couple, then the Lord will provide the mate she seeks. And all the give and take which is required will be by mutual consent and respect.

Daily Wisdom for Women

OCTOBER 2

ESTHER'S REQUEST

So Esther arose and stood before the king.

ESTHER 8:4

Esther and Mordecai were among the few in the king's palace who had acted in the king's behalf. Everyone else desired personal gain. Esther had risked her life not only for her people, but also for the king. Had it not been for God's intervention, Haman undoubtedly would have hanged Esther on that gallows right along with Mordecai.

One-Minute Meditations

3 OCTOBER

MICAH KNEW HIS GOD

The word of the Lord which came to Micah. . .Hear, O peoples, all of you; listen, O earth and all it contains, and let the Lord God be a witness against you, the Lord from His holy temple.

MICAH 1:1–2

Micah understood the Lord's awesome power. In fact, Micah's name means, "who is like Jehovah," forever reminding us that he understood the object of his faith. God used Micah to prophecy to the southern kingdom of Judah.

Daily Wisdom for Women

4 OCTOBER

THE PREACHER'S LIVELIHOOD

Who at any time serves as a soldier at his own expense?
Who plants a vineyard and does not eat the fruit of it?

1 CORINTHIANS 9:7

Those who bring us the Word of God deserve a living wage. The word apostle means "one sent under commission." And if they have been called into service by God, aren't they entitled to the financial support from the body of believers?

One-Minute Meditations

OCTOBER 5

The Reason for Job's Suffering

*Job. . .was blameless, upright,
fearing God and turning away from evil.*

Job 1:1

Satan intimated to God that Job only loved Him because of all the blessings Job had received. "Then the Lord said to Satan, 'Behold, all that he has is in your power, only do not put forth your hand on him' " (Job 1:12).

Daily Wisdom for Women

October 6

THE CONTENT OF OUR THOUGHTS

*Woe to those who scheme iniquity,
who work out evil on their beds!*

MICAH 2:1

Micah acknowledges that the source of evil thoughts is the human mind. Therein lies the problem, that we at some point begin to accept wickedness as good. And the things we devise in our minds then become the vehicle for our actions.

One-Minute Meditations

7 OCTOBER

God, Judge of Immorality Past and Present

*Now these things happened as examples for us,
so that we would not crave evil things.*

1 CORINTHIANS 10:6

How can we stop ourselves from falling into sin? By remembering: "No temptation has overtaken you but such as is common to man; and God is faithful, who will not allow you to be tempted beyond what you are able, but with the temptation will provide the way of escape also, so that you will be able to endure it" (1 Corinthians 10:13).

Daily Wisdom for Women

8 OCTOBER

A Little Help from His Friends

*"Remember now, who ever perished being innocent?
Or where were the upright destroyed?"*

Job 4:7

Just when things couldn't get worse, Job's friend, Eliphaz, drops a bomb at Job's feet: "For man is born for trouble, as sparks fly upward" (Job 5:7).

Do we stand on the bedrock of knowledge about God's goodness, despite the circumstances? Or do we succumb to the taunting of cruel and unfeeling friends?

One-Minute Meditations

9 OCTOBER

BETHLEHEM'S CHILD WILL RULE

And He will arise and shepherd His flock in the strength of the Lord, in the majesty of the name of the Lord His God.

MICAH 5:4

Christ's birth demanded worship or fear. After Jesus' birth the magi inquired of King Herod, "Where is He who has been born King of the Jews? For we saw His star in the east and have come to worship Him" (Matthew 2:2).

Daily Wisdom for Women

10 OCTOBER

The Holy Spirit, Our Great Gift

Therefore I make known to you that no one speaking by the Spirit of God says, "Jesus is accursed"; and no one can say, "Jesus is Lord," except by the Holy Spirit.

1 Corinthians 12:3

The evil one is the author of lies. Test the spirits. "By this you know the Spirit of God: every spirit that confesses that Jesus Christ has come in the flesh is from God (1 John 4:2).

One-Minute Meditations

**11
OCTOBER**

God Has "Been There, Done That"

"It is God who removes the mountains. . .who alone stretches out the heavens and tramples down the waves of the sea."

JOB 9:5, 8

As A.W. Tozer said, "We tend. . .to reduce God to manageable terms."

As our human nature cries out to control what we don't understand, this feat becomes impossible. For the God who has created all has "been there and done that."

When we accept this, our own importance seems diminished.

Daily Wisdom for Women

12 OCTOBER

What Response Does God Require?

*He has told you, O man, what is good; and what does the
LORD require of you but to do justice, to love kindness,
and to walk humbly with your God?*

MICAH 6:8

Christ has already paid the price for our sins. God looked upon our futility and became a man, and then He sacrificed His life so that we, who did not and could not ever deserve His mercy, might obtain it.

One-Minute Meditations

13 OCTOBER

How to Know If You're in Love

If I speak with the tongues of men and of angels, but do not have love, I have become a noisy gong or a clanging cymbal.

1 CORINTHIANS 13:1

Even though we've prayed for godly mates, and then relied on God's guidance, there will still be times when our attempts to love are less than perfect.

However, if both man and woman turn back to God's blueprint, harmony can be restored.

Daily Wisdom for Women

14 OCTOBER

True Environmentalists

"Who among all these does not know that the hand of the Lord has done this, in whose hand is the life of every living thing, and the breath of all mankind?"

JOB 12:9–10

The media regularly report how the earth's resources and species are diminishing rapidly. Perhaps we have forgotten that God also cares about every living thing. It's important to remember that Christ created animals for our enjoyment. Be grateful to the Lord.

One-Minute Meditations

15 OCTOBER

The True Shepherd Will Return

*Shepherd Your people with Your scepter,
the flock of Your possession which dwells by itself
in the woodland, in the midst of a fruitful field.*

MICAH 7:14

Jesus claimed to be the Good Shepherd. "I am the good shepherd" (John 10:11).

Furthermore, the Shepherd's return at the end of the age will be as judge. "For the Lamb in the center of the throne will be their shepherd, and will guide them to springs of the water of life" (Revelation 7:17).

Daily Wisdom for Women

16 OCTOBER

By One Man Death, By Another Man Life

But now Christ has been raised from the dead, the first fruits of those who are asleep. For since by a man came death, by a man also came the resurrection of the dead.

1 Corinthians 15:20–21

Satan would love to seduce us into thinking that Christ never rose from the dead. If that were the case, the whole foundation of our faith would crumble. For this reason, God inspired Paul to provide proof of the Resurrection.

One-Minute Meditations

17 OCTOBER

His Fortunes Restored

The LORD restored the fortunes of Job when he prayed for his friends, and the LORD increased all that Job had twofold.

JOB 42:10

Don't you just love stories with happy endings?

Finally, Job received the Lord's public vindication. Revenge doesn't get any sweeter than that! And don't you know that Eliphaz and Temanite were "sweatin' it big time" as they awaited Job's eloquent prayer that would restrain God's hand of wrath!

Daily Wisdom for Women

18 OCTOBER

Nahum Proclaims Israel's Restoration

Behold, on the mountains the feet of him who brings good news, who announces peace!

Nahum 1:15

Nahum knows that if God is presenting a message, then He's ready to take action. So Nahum, whose name means "comforter," is going to extol the virtues of His God to these pagans. That way, when God does begin His judgment, they'll know exactly whom they have encountered.

One-Minute Meditations

19 OCTOBER

WHEN WILL OUR SUFFERING CEASE?

*Blessed be the God and Father of our Lord Jesus Christ...
who comforts us...so that we will be able to
comfort those who are in any affliction.*

2 CORINTHIANS 1:3–4

This is the purpose of our trials, that we might comfort one another and lean on the Lord's strength. Paul's own burdens had been borne with a view of Christ that few of us will ever know.

Daily Wisdom for Women

20 OCTOBER

SLAVERY IS NOTHING NEW

*I appeal to you for my child Onesimus,
whom I have begotten in my imprisonment.*

PHILEMON 1:10

This passage provides a clear picture of what the Father did for each of us by sending His Son, Jesus Christ.

Paul became the beloved friend to both Philemon and Onesimus, not wishing for either to harm the other. He spoke to them heart-to-heart.

One-Minute Meditations

21 OCTOBER

What Is Your Foundation?

*"Woe to him who builds a city with bloodshed
and founds a town with violence!"*

HABAKKUK 2:12

Martin Luther was pierced by a verse in Habakkuk, and his reaction changed the course of church history. "The righteous will live by his faith" (Habakkuk 2:4). But in whom is this faith placed? If our faith is in Christ, we are established upon firm ground. But if it's in systems, programs, or even religion, it's doomed to fail.

Daily Wisdom for Women

22 OCTOBER

Paul's Trip to Paradise

On behalf of such a man I will boast; but on my own behalf I will not boast, except in regard to my weaknesses.

2 Corinthians 12:5

"To keep me from exalting myself, there was given me a thorn in the flesh" (2 Corinthians 12:7).

He never tells what that affliction was. But he did understand it as coming from the Lord. Paul chose not to dwell on his discomfort, clinging instead to the incredible and unforgettable things he saw and heard while in heaven.

One-Minute Meditations

23 OCTOBER

WE STILL HAVE A HIGH PRIEST

*When He had made purification of sins,
He sat down at the right hand of the Majesty on high.*

HEBREWS 1:3

Now God tabernacles among men, and Christ, God's perfect Lamb, has become our High Priest. "For we do not have a high priest who cannot sympathize with our weaknesses, but One who has been tempted in all things as we are, yet without sin" (Hebrews 4:15).

Daily Wisdom for Women

24 OCTOBER

Woe to the Mediocre!

*"Wail, O inhabitants of the Mortar,
for all the people of Canaan will be silenced."*

ZEPHANIAH 1:11

While the latest opinion polls show that a majority of us claim to believe in God, the crime rate soars, homosexuality is accepted as normal, and our teens search in vain for godly role models. How is faith evidenced?

This is the same question God was posing to Israel. And as surely as judgment fell upon them, it will ultimately fall on us.

One-Minute Meditations

25 OCTOBER

Grace Versus the Law

I am amazed that you are so quickly deserting Him who called you by the grace of Christ.

Galatians 1:6

Jewish believers were transitioning from the Law, filled with regulations, and beginning to follow the gospel of grace. However, they easily fell into the trap of "desiring their old robes back."

Therefore, Paul left on his missionary journeys to bring the gospel of grace to those who were being seduced by this group.

Daily Wisdom for Women

26 OCTOBER

Heart Prompting

Therefore, holy brethren, partakers of a heavenly calling, consider Jesus, the Apostle and High Priest of our confession.

Hebrews 3:1

Do you ever wake up thinking about someone you may not have seen in years? God may be prompting your heart to respond to that person's need for encouragement.

One of Paul's great gifts was that of being an encourager. Yes, he spoke the truth unabashedly, yet he tempered it with praise and hope.

One-Minute Meditations

27 OCTOBER

A Day of Prayer

*Seek righteousness, seek humility.
Perhaps you will be hidden in the day of the LORD's anger.*

ZEPHANIAH 2:3

The majority of Zephaniah's audience will perish instead of listening with their hearts. Only a faithful few will be spared.

The remnant which survived, long into Israel's future, saw the day of this prophecy's fulfillment. "Shout in triumph, O daughter of Jerusalem! Behold, your king is coming to you; He is just and endowed with salvation, humble" (Zechariah 9:9).

Daily Wisdom for Women

28 OCTOBER

For What Are You Zealous?

*For am I now seeking the favor of men, or of God?
Or am I striving to please men? If I were still trying to please men,
I would not be a bond-servant of Christ.*

GALATIANS 1:10

Paul didn't sit around asking men for their opinions. Christ's call was sufficient. Therefore, he devoted himself to study, prayer, and meditation alone with his Lord.

One-Minute Meditations

29 OCTOBER

Who Is the Rightful Heir?

*Abraham had two sons, one by the
bondwoman and one by the free woman.*

GALATIANS 4:22

Paul now uses these two sons to illustrate the status of the unbeliever versus her changed relationship once she commits her life to Christ. Once we were slaves to sin. But with our redemption in Christ, we become free.

Daily Wisdom for Women

30 OCTOBER

Get Those Hammers Ready

*"Thus says the Lord of hosts, 'This people says,
"The time has not come, even the time for
the house of the Lord to be rebuilt."'"*

Haggai 1:2

Although a small remnant had begun rebuilding, they had become overwhelmed. Now God commissioned Haggai to bring His motivating Word to the people.

The task loomed larger than life so the Lord spoke again: " 'Take courage,' declares the Lord, 'and work; for I am with you' " (Haggai 2:4).

One-Minute Meditations

31 OCTOBER

HALLOWEEN, DAY OF EVIL OR INNOCENT FUN?

Therefore, let us fear if, while a promise remains of entering His rest, any one of you may seem to have come short of it.

HEBREWS 4:1

To go along with the "harvest festival" idea already fostered by many churches, is a drama book by Louis Merryman entitled *Halloween Alternatives*, containing ideas for reaching young minds with the gospel.

Today's scripture is about "entering into God's rest," something which those who do not choose Him will never experience.

Daily Wisdom for Women

1 NOVEMBER

MELCHIZEDEK, PRIEST OF THE MOST HIGH GOD

For this Melchizedek, king of Salem, priest of the Most High God. . . made like the Son of God, he remains a priest perpetually.

HEBREWS 7:1, 3

Melchizedek is first mentioned in Genesis. This priest of the Most High God came out to meet Abraham and introduced himself as a priest of God Most High (Genesis 14:17–24). Abraham affirmed this king-priest by giving Melchizedek tithes and also receiving the blessing he gave.

One-Minute Meditations

2 NOVEMBER

Zechariah, Messenger of the Messiah's Triumph

"These are those whom the LORD has sent to patrol the earth."

ZECHARIAH 1:10

Zechariah's name means "God remembers." The message he received from the Lord came when Israel most needed to be reminded that their God still stood watch over them. Only a remnant of them had returned from the Babylonian captivity.

Through a series of eight visions, God unfolds His future plans for Israel and the completion of the temple to Zechariah.

Daily Wisdom for Women

3 NOVEMBER

The Fruit of the Spirit

But the fruit of the Spirit is love, joy, peace, patience, kindness, goodness, faithfulness, gentleness, self-control; against such things there is no law.

GALATIANS 5:22–23

Inventoried in today's scripture are qualities that, apart from God's power, would likely not be displayed in our character.

Why is God showering us with these gifts? Because they prove that He can enter a human life and affect her with change, that others might also be won to Christ.

One-Minute Meditations

4 NOVEMBER

JAMES, BOND-SERVANT OF GOD

James, a bond-servant of God and of the Lord Jesus Christ...

JAMES 1:1

James finally understood his position in Christ, that of a servant. He had successfully journeyed from a place of hindering the gospel, unaware of the time constraints Christ had with the Father, to a place of understanding the true source of wisdom. Paul relates that James, along with Peter and John, became one of the chief leaders of the church in Jerusalem.

Daily Wisdom for Women

5 NOVEMBER

THE DIVINE PROTECTOR OF JERUSALEM

"Jerusalem will be inhabited without walls because of the multitude of men and cattle within it."

ZECHARIAH 2:4

At a time when only a remnant of Israel had returned to Jerusalem, the Lord is promising that at a future time they will become a great nation, having grown so large that conventional walls will be obsolete. Zechariah is being told that someday in the future, walls won't be necessary.

One-Minute Meditations

6 NOVEMBER

Chosen Before the Foundation of the World

He chose us in Him before the foundation of the world, that we would be holy and blameless before Him.

Ephesians 1:4

When God created the world He not only planned your place in it, but He also reserved a place in heaven for you. Now, you can either claim your ticket by accepting Christ's salvation on your behalf, or you can cancel the reservation by never responding to God's offer.

Daily Wisdom for Women

NOVEMBER 7

WHAT CONSTITUTES DYNAMIC FAITH?

"AND ABRAHAM BELIEVED GOD, AND IT WAS RECKONED TO HIM AS RIGHTEOUSNESS," and he was called the friend of God.

JAMES 2:23

Abraham's faith was evident by his actions. The very foundation of Abraham's faith was the Word of God. And no matter what God required of him, Abraham obeyed God. Therefore, all of his actions were born out of the call God had on his life.

One-Minute Meditations

8 NOVEMBER

THE "HOLY LAND" OF CHRIST'S RETURN

"The Lord will possess Judah as His portion in the holy land, and will again choose Jerusalem."

ZECHARIAH 2:12

True holiness cannot reign within Israel until the Messiah, Jesus Christ, comes to inhabit this nation. At present, Israel is a secular, humanistic country. However, the future holds for Israel a time when the Lord Jesus Christ will reign from Jerusalem as King.

Daily Wisdom for Women

9 NOVEMBER

SEALED BY THE HOLY SPIRIT

In Him, you also, after listening to the message of truth, the gospel of your salvation—having also believed, you were sealed in Him with the Holy Spirit of promise.

EPHESIANS 1:13

Ornamental sealing waxes and metal impressions were used in the past as both a security measure and a statement of authenticity. Paul was inspired to use this image to describe how we, as believers, are sealed by God's Holy Spirit.

One-Minute Meditations

10 NOVEMBER

Oh, That "Biting Tongue"

*And the tongue is a fire, the very world of iniquity;
the tongue is set among our members as that which defiles the entire body.*

JAMES 3:6

We all have difficulty either saying too much or not saying it right. I can remember one of my former Bible study leaders saying, "If your second remark is usually an apology for your first remark, you've got a problem!"

Daily Wisdom for Women

NOVEMBER 11

Israel's Filthy Garments

*Now Joshua was clothed with filthy garments
and standing before the angel.*

Zechariah 3:3

Joshua is wearing robes that are filthy as a symbol of Israel's sins that need to be cleansed by God.

How can God go on loving them? The same way He continues to love us. He has provided the means for our atonement and will do all in His power to lead us to the cross that we might obtain it.

One-Minute Meditations

12 NOVEMBER

A Husband's Love

*But as the church is subject to Christ,
so also the wives ought to be to their husbands in everything.*

EPHESIANS 5:24

Wives, our role is that of a helpmate, not doormat. It's critical to remember that God intended marriage to be a partnership. Pray. . .every single day. Know that God is vitally interested in the success of your marriage and act accordingly.

Daily Wisdom for Women

13 NOVEMBER

PETER, AN APOSTLE OF JESUS CHRIST

Peter, an apostle of Jesus Christ, to those who reside as aliens...

1 PETER 1:1

The only true "superhero" is Jesus Christ, who will never fail us. To credit Peter with a more elevated status than the one given to him by Christ is to add to the scriptures. Peter never seeks position or power. Instead, he humbly admonishes his hearers to "obey Christ," on whom Peter also depends.

One-Minute Meditations

14 NOVEMBER

A Closer Walk with Thee

*"If you will walk in My ways. . .then you will also govern
My house and also have charge of My courts, and I will grant
you free access among these who are standing here."*

ZECHARIAH 3:7

As incredible an offer as this might have been for Joshua, an even more miraculous invitation awaits those who accept Jesus as their Lord and Savior. Immediately, they can enjoy the presence of God every day of their lives.

Daily Wisdom for Women

15 NOVEMBER

THE MEANING OF TRUE CHRISTIAN FELLOWSHIP

*I thank my God in all my remembrance of you,
always offering prayer with joy in my every prayer for you all,
in view of your participation in the gospel from the first day until now.*

PHILIPPIANS 1:3–5

Paul's joy is not dependent upon circumstances. Rather, it overflows from the content of his heart, where the true source of joy resides, Jesus Christ. And because of this indwelling, Paul senses a oneness with other believers.

One-Minute Meditations

16 NOVEMBER

Born Again to a Living Hope

In this you greatly rejoice, even though now for a little while, if necessary, you have been distressed by various trials, so that the proof of your faith. . .may be found to result in praise and glory and honor at the revelation of Jesus Christ.

1 Peter 1:6–7

What degree of persecution are you willing to endure that the gospel of truth might go forward to a needy world?

Daily Wisdom for Women

17 NOVEMBER

Our Precious Cornerstone

*"For behold, the stone that I have set before Joshua;
on one stone are seven eyes."*

Zechariah 3:9

The rock which Zechariah describes here is Jesus Christ. Daniel described Him as a "stone [which] was cut out of the mountain without hands and that it crushed the iron, the bronze, the clay, the silver and the gold" (Daniel 2:45).

The Psalms present the Messiah as "the stone which the builders rejected" (Psalm 118:22).

Isaiah 28:16 describes the Messiah as the foundation stone.

One-Minute Meditations

18 NOVEMBER

BEING OF ONE MIND

*Do nothing from selfishness or empty conceit,
but with humility of mind regard one another
as more important than yourselves.*

PHILIPPIANS 2:3

As Christians we are called to encourage one another in the faith. Paul had a deep understanding of the need for the reassurance and hope which the Lord richly supplied. This reliance on God's abundant source of blessings overflowed from his heart, spilling out to his fellow Christians.

Daily Wisdom for Women

19 NOVEMBER

BABES IN CHRIST

*Like newborn babies, long for the pure milk of the word,
so that by it you may grow in respect to salvation,
if you have tasted the kindness of the Lord.*

1 PETER 2:2–3

As mothers, grandmothers, stepmothers, and aunts, we have a God-ordained call to teach children the Word of God that they might someday enter the kingdom of God.

One-Minute Meditations

20 NOVEMBER

God's Glory, the Menorah of Heaven

*He said to me, "What do you see?"
And I said, "I see, and behold, a lampstand all
of gold with its bowl on the top of it."*

ZECHARIAH 4:2

God's purpose for these visions was to prompt Zechariah to motivate the Israelites to rebuild the temple. The Lord was showing him the symbolism behind the earthly temple, which is a replica of the one God has in heaven.

Daily Wisdom for Women

21 NOVEMBER

STAND FIRM AND RECEIVE THE CROWN

Stand firm in the Lord.... I urge Euodia and I urge Syntyche to live in harmony in the Lord.

PHILIPPIANS 4:1–2

Perhaps you have encountered someone who, although she professes belief in Christ, has treated you without charity or love. Fast, pray for guidance, and then go to her and pray again. Failure to do so gives Satan an opportunity to get a foothold within the church, as the argument escalates and people choose sides.

One-Minute Meditations

NOVEMBER 22

Should You Leave an Unbelieving Husband?

In the same way, you wives, be submissive to your own husbands so that. . .they may be won.

1 Peter 3:1

I was a Christian for thirteen years before my husband made his own commitment. These were extremely difficult times. However, they also included the cultivation of my own relationship with the Lord, as Bible study became a matter of daily survival. When my husband "saw the light," he had a family that already knew the Lord.

Daily Wisdom for Women

23 NOVEMBER

Two Olive Branches

Then I said to him, "What are these two olive trees on the right of the lampstand and on its left?"

ZECHARIAH 4:11

While they are symbolically referred to as "olive branches," these are two men who spread the gospel to the Jews during the tribulation period. They have God's authority to speak as His prophets during one of the most trying periods of time in history.

One-Minute Meditations

24 NOVEMBER

Giving Thanks to God

We give thanks to God, the Father of our Lord Jesus Christ, praying always for you, since we heard of your faith in Christ Jesus and the love which you have for all the saints.

Colossians 1:3–4

Paul reaches out to this nucleus of believers with God's truth that their foundation in Him might remain strong enough to withstand the bombardment of confusing thoughts which tore at them daily.

Daily Wisdom for Women

25 NOVEMBER

God's Precious Promises

His divine power has granted to us everything pertaining to life and godliness, through the true knowledge of Him who called us.

2 Peter 1:3

From the moment a baby is conceived, it has everything it needs to grow into a complete human being. Our spiritual growth is the same. From the moment we accept Christ, He infuses His Spirit within us, giving us right-standing with the Father and making us a child of God.

One-Minute Meditations

**26
NOVEMBER**

God Questions Israel's Motive for Rituals

"When you fasted and mourned in the fifth and seventh months these seventy years, was it actually for Me that you fasted?"

Zechariah 7:5

The Lord instituted several feasts for Israel to commemorate important events during which He had delivered their nation.

Instead, the Israelites had made nothing but rituals out of the days. They questioned whether they needed to continue observing them.

Daily Wisdom for Women

27 NOVEMBER

The Image of the Invisible God

He is the image of the invisible God, the firstborn of all creation.

Colossians 1:15

The entire Bible presents a singular message about Christ's identity. The first verse of Genesis says it all: "In the beginning God created the heavens and the earth" (Genesis 1:1). The word for God in this passage is Elohim and it's plural—for there are three distinct persons within the Godhead—the Father, Son, and Holy Spirit.

One-Minute Meditations

28
NOVEMBER

Where Is the Promise of His Coming?

"Where is the promise of His coming?"

2 Peter 3:4

How can a loving God destroy the very men and women and their world which He created? Look at how much time He provided for them to repent. From the time Noah received the order from God to build the ark until the rain began, a span of 120 years had elapsed. Certainly this was time enough for everyone to hear the prediction and take appropriate action.

Daily Wisdom for Women

29 NOVEMBER

God Stands by His Word

"And the Lord, whom you seek, will suddenly come to His temple."

MALACHI 3:1

Today's scripture reveals a specific message. The Messiah will "come to His temple." Later Christ stood in the temple and read from the book of Isaiah the very prophecy concerning His coming. Then He said, "Today this scripture has been fulfilled in your hearing" (Luke 4:21).

One-Minute Meditations

30 NOVEMBER

HOLD TO GOD'S TRUTH, NOT TO VISIONS

*You have died and your life is hidden with Christ in God.
When Christ, who is our life, is revealed,
then you also will be revealed with Him in glory.*

COLOSSIANS 3:3–4

Paul's message is that Christ in us should cause a change in our lives. For we have been delivered from the "wrath of God," (Colossians 3:6). This metamorphosis should make a visible difference in how we are living our lives. For Christ has set up residence within us.

Daily Wisdom for Women

1 DECEMBER

CHRISTMAS JOY

What we have seen and heard we proclaim to you also, so that you too may have fellowship with us; and indeed our fellowship is with the Father, and with His Son Jesus Christ.

1 JOHN 1:3

Are your cards in the mail yet?

Consider today what printed message you will send to loved ones this Christmas. . .a message of hope about Christ the Savior, or a scene in which He is nowhere to be found?

One-Minute Meditations

2 DECEMBER

The Revelation of Jesus Christ

The Revelation of Jesus Christ, which God gave Him to show to His bond-servants, the things which must soon take place…

Revelation 1:1

To those seeking to add further revelations to what God had pronounced as complete, God has issued a warning (see Revelation 22:18). So, if someone comes to your door and tries to hand you "another gospel" or "further revelations," you don't even need to read it to be assured that it is false.

Daily Wisdom for Women

3 DECEMBER

Christ Eliminated All Ethnic Barriers

There is no distinction between Greek and Jew, circumcised and uncircumcised, barbarian, Scythian, slave and freeman, but Christ is all, and in all.

COLOSSIANS 3:11

To say we love Christ and yet maintain deeply rooted prejudices against others is inconsistent with everything He taught. For Christ came to reconcile all peoples to Himself, not separate us into factions.

One-Minute Meditations

4 DECEMBER

The Father Has Bestowed a Great Love

Beloved, now we are children of God, and it has not appeared as yet what we will be. We know that when He appears, we will be like Him, because we will see Him just as He is.

1 JOHN 3:2

The gift of our new bodies is only one aspect of the Father's incredible love for His children. His love prompts His children to purify themselves just as He is pure. They also abide in Him and practice righteousness, for they have been born of God.

Daily Wisdom for Women

5 DECEMBER

HE IS COMING WITH THE CLOUDS

BEHOLD, HE IS COMING WITH THE CLOUDS, and every eye will see Him, even those who pierced Him; and all the tribes of the earth will mourn over Him. So it is to be. Amen.

REVELATION 1:7

This future event will be a worldwide phenomenon in which every eye will see Him. The purpose for His appearance this time will be to judge the world of its greatest sin, the rejection of His great gift of salvation.

One-Minute Meditations

6 DECEMBER

How the Church Was Born

*...constantly bearing in mind your work of faith and labor of love
and steadfastness of hope in our Lord Jesus Christ
in the presence of our God and Father.*

1 THESSALONIANS 1:3

God meant for His Church to be dynamic. This is the place where His believers gather to worship and grow. Paul and his little band of followers gave their lives to start churches founded and grounded in the Word of God.

Daily Wisdom for Women

7 DECEMBER

SPIRIT OF GOD OR SPIRIT OF THE ANTICHRIST?

The eyes of the LORD are toward the righteous and His ears are open to their cry.

PSALM 34:15

The Spirit of God heard my cry and took my petition before the Father who answered my prayer, for I have confessed belief in Him.

Let God guide in this last hour, that you continue to spread the gospel and not walk away.

One-Minute Meditations

8 DECEMBER

God's Message to the Churches

"But I have this against you, that you have left your first love."

REVELATION 2:4

There is nothing to compare with that "first bloom of love." .

This is the kind of love which God desires from us. That on-fire, totally consuming, single focus of our attention. His call to the church at Ephesus then was that they remember their first love—and rekindle their purpose to seek Him first.

Daily Wisdom for Women

DECEMBER 9

PRECISE INSTRUCTIONS TO THE BELOVED

But examine everything carefully; hold fast to that which is good; abstain from every form of evil.

1 THESSALONIANS 5:21–22

This encouraging letter provides Paul's spiritual last will, recording a priority list of ways in which we can live out the gospel of Christ.

For God equates love with obedience. When Christ returns for His believers, we are to be found walking in His statutes.

One-Minute Meditations

10 DECEMBER

Those Born of God Obey Him

By this we know that we love the children of God, when we love God and observe His commandments.

1 JOHN 5:2

When our children disobey, we feel not only extreme disappointment but a sense that they don't love us. For if they did, they would understand that our instructions are meant to guide them over the rough terrain of life. This is exactly how God feels when we fail to follow Him. For He equates love with obedience.

Daily Wisdom for Women

11 DECEMBER

THE RAINBOW SURROUNDING CHRIST

*And there was a rainbow around the throne,
like an emerald in appearance.*

REVELATION 4:3

We see that there is a rainbow in heaven, but it's not the half-bow we're used to seeing. This rainbow is a complete circle because in heaven all things are whole and finished. Yet the most amazing thing about this prism of color is that it surrounds Christ.

We know this because there He is "sitting on the throne" (Revelation 4:2), which is the posture of judgment.

One-Minute Meditations

12 DECEMBER

WHEN WILL CHRIST RAPTURE THE FAITHFUL?

*Now we request you, brethren, with regard to the coming of our
Lord Jesus Christ and our gathering together to Him,
that you not be quickly shaken from your composure.*

2 THESSALONIANS 2:1–2

Before the Antichrist bursts onto the world scene, there will be a great falling away from the truth: "Some will fall away from the faith, paying attention to deceitful spirits and doctrines of demons" (1 Timothy 4:1).

Daily Wisdom for Women

13 DECEMBER

THE FATHER HAS COMMANDED US TO LOVE

The elder to the chosen lady and her children, whom I love in truth; and not only I, but also all who know the truth. . .

2 JOHN 1:1

A foundation of any small-group home Bible study should be the love members display toward one another. It was just such a group which John addressed in this letter.

As a church elder, John reminded these believers that God didn't consider loving one another an option.

One-Minute Meditations

14 DECEMBER

Jesus Alone Is Worthy

"Stop weeping; behold, the Lion that is from the tribe of Judah, the Root of David, has overcome so as to open the book and its seven seals."

REVELATION 5:5

As the Lamb stood to receive "the book," an awed hush fell over His celestial audience. For He alone was worthy, because He had met God's requirements to redeem the earth. The prize was His.

Daily Wisdom for Women

15 DECEMBER

Jesus Christ, Our Hope

But the goal of our instruction is love from a pure heart and a good conscience and a sincere faith.

1 Timothy 1:5

Paul wrote this letter to encourage Timothy in his own leadership role, knowing that the worst thing this young believer could do was to try to emulate Paul instead of Christ.

Timothy is his "true child in the faith" (1 Timothy 1:2), for Paul had led him to Christ and never ceased to pray for his spiritual growth.

One-Minute Meditations

16 DECEMBER

Jesus Christ Came in the Flesh

If anyone comes to you and does not bring this teaching, do not receive him into your house.

2 JOHN 1:10

There is no greater evil than to fail to recognize who Jesus Christ is: God in the flesh. God sent Jesus to show us how to live upon the earth. And instead of responding to His offer of salvation, men nailed Him to a cross.

Today's scripture warns against false teachings.

Daily Wisdom for Women

17 DECEMBER

The Lamb Breaks Three Seals

Behold, a white horse. . .and another, a red horse. . . and behold, a black horse.

REVELATION 6:2, 4–5

Each of these three horsemen represents a judgment that will come upon the earth. The first rider, on a white horse, has a bow, but notice he doesn't have any arrows. The next rider, on a red horse, is granted permission to "take peace from the earth" (Revelation 6:4). The third rider, sitting atop a black horse, holds "a pair of scales" (Revelation 6:5). This reveals that famine will accompany the war.

One-Minute Meditations

18 DECEMBER

Order in Our Prayers

First of all, then, I urge that entreaties and prayers, petitions and thanksgivings, be made on behalf of all men.

1 Timothy 2:1

Prayer isn't some mystical entity to be attained by a few saintly little ladies in the church. Instead, it is an act of worship on the part of the created toward the Creator. Prayer is simply talking to God about everything that affects our lives.

Daily Wisdom for Women

19 DECEMBER

WELCOMING OTHER BELIEVERS

Beloved, you are acting faithfully in whatever you accomplish for the brethren, and especially when they are strangers.

3 JOHN 1:5

It was the truth to which Gaius was a witness that had molded this extraordinary life, one centered on obedience to God. Gaius provided genuine hospitality. And evidently this included opening his own home, heart, and pocketbook to others, that the Word of God might go forth.

One-Minute Meditations

20 DECEMBER

THREE MORE SEALS ARE OPENED

When the Lamb broke the fourth seal. . .I looked, and behold, an ashen horse; and he who sat on it had the name Death; and Hades was following with him.

REVELATION 6:7–8

In this vision John viewed two personages. First came Death, the rider of the pale horse, and Hades followed him. Although Death claims the body and Hades the soul, only Jesus Christ holds the keys of Death and Hades.

Daily Wisdom for Women

21 DECEMBER

Timothy: Fit for Leadership

It is a trustworthy statement: if any man aspires to the office of overseer, it is a fine work he desires to do. An overseer, then, must be above reproach, the husband of one wife, temperate, prudent, respectable, hospitable.

1 Timothy 3:1–2

An overseer refers to one who held the primary responsibility of directing the work of the church. Such a man was to lead a blameless life, that his character would never be in question (1 Timothy 3:2).

One-Minute Meditations

22 DECEMBER

God's Bond-Servants Are Sealed

"Do not harm the earth or the sea or the trees until we have sealed the bond-servants of our God on their foreheads."

REVELATION 7:3

After centuries upon centuries of enduring Israel's disobedience and broken promises, God still loves His people. And He's about to preserve for Himself "a remnant" of the nation who will survive the atrocities of the tribulation.

Daily Wisdom for Women

23 DECEMBER

Paul's Ministry Comes to a Close

I constantly remember you in my prayers night and day, longing to see you, even as I recall your tears, so that I may be filled with joy. For I am mindful of the sincere faith within you.

2 Timothy 1:3–5

Paul had to make sure that Timothy, who suffered from bouts of insecurity, remained strong in the faith. For Timothy would now carry the torch of faith and continue bringing the gospel to all who would listen.

One-Minute Meditations

24 DECEMBER

Jude, a Bond-Servant of Jesus Christ

Beloved, while I was making every effort to write you about our common salvation, I felt the necessity to write to you appealing that you contend earnestly for the faith which was once for all handed down to the saints.

JUDE 1:3

Jude writes to exhort the "saints," those who are sanctified or "set apart" by God, reminding them that they share salvation in Christ.

Daily Wisdom for Women

25 DECEMBER

Happy Birthday, Jesus!

And she gave birth to her firstborn son; and she wrapped Him in cloths, and laid Him in a manger, because there was no room for them in the inn.

LUKE 2:7

Joy fills our hearts as we celebrate Christmas. Are we mindful of the sacrifices surrounding this Savior's birth? Christ, the Son of God, willingly left heaven's throne, took on a human body, and grew to manhood so He could die on the cross.

One-Minute Meditations

26 DECEMBER

Titus, Appointed by Paul

*Paul, a bond-servant of God and
an apostle of Jesus Christ. . . to Titus. . .*

Titus 1:1, 4

After Paul had made sure that Timothy was well-grounded, he turned his attention to Titus, in Crete.

Paul's letter to Titus is similar to the one he wrote to Timothy. The qualities for choosing leaders is so critical that Paul makes sure nothing is left unclear.

He also admonishes the older people to hold fast to the truth (Titus 2:2–5).

Daily Wisdom for Women

27 DECEMBER

God's Voice of Truth

"And I will grant authority to my two witnesses."

REVELATION 11:3

God appoints two witnesses who speak forth His word for 1,260 days. The "saints of God" have been taken to heaven, and the Holy Spirit has been taken out of the world. Those choosing to remain in unbelief become terrified of the two witnesses, for their God-given power is truly awesome!

One-Minute Meditations

28 DECEMBER

THE MARRIAGE SUPPER OF THE LAMB

"Let us rejoice and be glad and give the glory to Him, for the marriage of the Lamb has come and His bride has made herself ready."

REVELATION 19:7

John the Apostle reveals Christ again as the Lamb. He is preparing a supper in which His bride, the Church, will be in the presence of the Lamb. This scene will take place in heaven, where the believers finally see Christ face-to-face.

Daily Wisdom for Women

29 DECEMBER

The Eternal Gospel

*And I saw another angel flying in midheaven,
having an eternal gospel to preach to those who live on the earth,
and to every nation and tribe and tongue and people.*

Revelation 14:6

Following the Resurrection, Jesus prepared to leave this earth and return to heaven. Before going, He delivered a message to His disciples and charged them with a mission.

This great commission is extended to all who choose to believe in Christ.

One-Minute Meditations

30 DECEMBER

Some Will Be Singing

*And they sang the song of Moses,
the bond-servant of God, and the song of the Lamb.*

REVELATION 15:3

Those who are victorious over the adversities of the last days on earth will have much to celebrate. This victorious number will include many Jews who come to believe in Christ as their Messiah. And in true Israelite fashion, they will express their jubilation in song.

Daily Wisdom for Women

31 DECEMBER

We Shall Behold Him

There will no longer be any curse; and the throne of God and of the Lamb will be in it.

REVELATION 22:3

In the garden, God promised Adam and Eve that He would send a Redeemer. This Redeemer would die on the cross for our sins.

God is presenting you with a chance for a fresh start. Today you can take the first step that leads to Jesus. Will you choose to behold Him. . .face-to-face?

Scripture Index

Genesis
 1:27—1/1
 3:6—1/2
 9:13—1/4
 17:16—1/7
 18:20—1/10
 39:6–8—1/19
 45:5—1/24
 46:4—1/23

Exodus
 3:11—1/26
 4:10—1/29
 9:27—1/30
 12:21, 23—2/2
 13:20–21—2/3
 20:8—2/5
 28:4—2/8
 35:21—2/11

Leviticus
 1:2—2/14
 11:2—2/19

 20:8—2/24
 25:11—2/27

Numbers
 1:2–3—3/2
 6:2–3—3/4
 12:5, 8—3/8
 16:1, 3—3/10
 19:5—3/13
 25:4—3/16
 26:52–53—3/18
 33:1, 3—3/21
 36:8—3/22

Deuteronomy
 1:13—3/26
 6:4—3/29
 18:10—3/31
 28:15—4/3
 30:6—4/5
 31:7—4/7
 34:9—4/11

Joshua

2:1—4/14
4:3—4/18
6:2—4/20
10:13—4/24
14:1—4/28

Judges

1:1—4/30
2:2—5/5
3:12—5/7
4:4–5—5/11
4:14—5/12
6:12—5/17
7:2—5/22
9:2—5/26
11:1—5/29
12:8–10—6/1
13:3—6/4
13:24—6/7
16:4—6/10

Ruth

1:4—6/13

1 Samuel

1:10—6/14
1:20—6/17
2:1—6/20
2:28–29—6/23
3:4—6/26
4:11—7/1
8:3—7/2
9:2—7/7
9:16—7/10
16:1—7/13
17:26—7/16
24:10—7/19
31:2—7/22

2 Samuel

1:4—7/25
2:4—7/28
7:3—7/31

11:2—8/3
12:14—8/6
22:2—8/9

1 Kings
2:4—8/12
3:9—8/15

2 Kings
2:1—8/18
17:16, 18—8/21

1 Chronicles
21:22—8/24

2 Chronicles
1:14—8/27
29:1–2—8/30

Ezra
1:3—9/2
4:4—9/5
4:17—9/8

Nehemiah
1:4—9/11
8:3—9/14

Esther
1:2–3—9/17
2:2, 4—9/20
2:22—9/23
3:13—9/26
5:8—9/29
8:4—10/2

Job
1:1—10/5
4:7—10/8
9:5, 8—10/11
12:9–10—10/14
42:10—10/17

Psalms
5:3—1/6
10:16—1/14
11:7—1/15
12:1—1/16

18:16, 18—1/22
22:1—1/28
30:11—2/6
34:15—12/7
39:5—2/21
51:5—3/7
56:4—3/14
61:1–3—3/20
66:1–2—3/24
68:5—3/28
71:3—4/2
78:1–2—4/6
79:9—4/12
83:4—4/13
84:2—4/22
86:8, 10—4/27
92:1—5/2
105:40—5/8
110:1—5/13
118:22—5/15
119:26–27—5/19
139:13–14—5/23
139:14—2/20
150:6—5/27

Proverbs
1:5—1/3
2:6—1/9
6:12–14—2/1
8:1–3—2/7
8:22—2/10
9:13–15—2/16
10:7—2/28
10:8–9—2/22
10:30—3/6
13:3—4/26
13:24—4/9
14:1—5/3
14:33—5/6
16:3—5/10
15:25—5/16
18:3—5/20
31:10–12—5/24

Ecclesiastes
1:2—5/30
2:1—6/2
3:1, 4—6/8
11:5—6/5

12:1—6/11

SONG OF SOLOMON
2:13—6/15

ISAIAH
1:2–3—6/18
1:10—6/21
2:6—6/24
7:14—6/27
9:2—1/17
13:6—6/29
40:5—7/4
62:2—7/5
66:1—7/8

JEREMIAH
1:5—7/11
1:16—7/14
3:18—7/17
50:34—7/20

LAMENTATIONS
2:5—7/23

EZEKIEL
1:1—7/26
3:4—7/29
3:12—8/1
5:11—8/4
13:9–10—8/7

DANIEL
1:12—8/10
3:4–5—8/13
6:4—8/16
7:1, 3—8/19
9:24—8/22
10:12—8/25
11:21—8/28
12:1—8/31

HOSEA
1:2–3—9/3
14:4—9/6

JOEL
1:4—9/9
3:11—9/12

Amos
1:3—9/15

Obadiah
1:15—9/18

Jonah
1:3—9/21
1:12—9/24
2:7—9/27
3:10—9/30

Micah
1:1–2—10/3
2:1—10/6
5:4—10/9
6:8—10/12
7:14—10/15

Nahum
1:15—10/18

Habakkuk
2:12—10/21

Zephaniah
1:11—10/24
2:3—10/27

Haggai
1:2—10/30

Zechariah
1:10—11/2
2:4—11/5
2:12—11/8
3:3—11/11
3:7—11/14
3:9—11/17
4:2—11/20
4:11—11/23
7:5—11/26

Malachi
3:1—11/29

Matthew
4:19—1/5
6:7—1/8

7:14—1/11
7:15–16—1/12
8:25—1/13
10:32—1/18
13:10—1/20
13:54—1/21
16:11—1/25
16:15–16—1/27
19:28—1/31
22:2—2/4
26:33—2/9
27:30–31—2/12

Mark

1:10—2/13
1:31—2/15
3:33, 35—2/17
5:28—2/18
7:25—2/23
9:2–3—2/25
10:7–9—2/26
10:15—4/19
10:34—3/1
11:28—3/3

12:38, 40—3/5
14:51, 53—3/9
15:11—3/11
15:43—3/12

Luke

1:7—3/15
2:7—12/25
2:36–37—3/17
3:3—3/19
4:3—3/23
5:27–29—3/25
6:12–13—3/27
9:2—3/30
9:30–31—4/1
10:39–40—4/4
12:9—4/8
13:34—4/10
15:9–10—4/16
16:23—4/17
17:3—4/21
18:31—4/23
18:2—4/25
19:30—4/29

John
1:1—5/1
1:14—5/4
1:21—5/9
1:41—5/14
2:3—5/18
3:3—5/21
3:36—5/25
4:7—5/28
5:4—5/31
6:58—6/3
7:5—6/6
8:4-5—6/9
9:1—6/12
10:3—6/16
11:1, 3—6/19
12:3—6/22
12:46—6/25
13:4-5—6/28
14:2—6/30
15:5—7/3
16:8—7/6
17:4—7/9
18:2—7/12
18:21—7/15
19:1-2—7/21
19:22—7/18
20:2—7/24
21:4—7/27

Acts
1:5—7/30
2:1, 4—8/2
2:33—8/5
2:38—8/11
3:18-19—8/14
4:8, 12—8/8
8:1—8/17
12:1-2—8/20
18:3—8/23

Romans
1:1—8/26
2:3—8/29
4:3—9/1
5:1—9/4
8:2-3—9/7
10:1—9/10

12:1—9/13
13:1, 6—4/15
16:1–2 — 9/16

1 Corinthians
1:2—9/19
2:10—9/22
3:16—9/25
6:2—9/28
7:3—10/1
9:7—10/4
10:6—10/7
12:3—10/10
13:1—10/13
15:20–21—10/16

2 Corinthians
1:3–4—10/19
12:5—10/22

Galatians
1:6—10/25
1:10—10/28
4:22—10/29

5:22–23—11/3

Ephesians
1:4—11/6
1:13—11/9
5:24—11/12

Philippians
1:3–5—11/15
2:3—11/18
4:1–2—11/21

Colossians
1:3–4—11/24
1:15—11/27
3:3–4—11/30
3:11—12/3

1 Thessalonians
1:3—12/6
5:21–22—12/9

2 Thessalonians
2:1–2—12/12

1 Timothy
1:5—12/15
2:1—12/18
3:1–2—12/21

2 Timothy
1:3–5—12/23

Titus
1:1, 4—12/26

Philemon
1:10—10/20

Hebrews
1:3—10/23
3:1—10/26
4:1—10/31
7:1, 3—11/1

James
1:1—11/4
2:23—11/7
3:6—11/10

1 Peter
1:1—11/13
1:6–7—11/16
2:2–3—11/19
3:1—11/22

2 Peter
1:3—11/25
3:4—11/28

1 John
1:3—12/1
3:2—12/4
5:2—12/10

2 John
1:1—12/13
1:10—12/16

3 John
1:5—12/19

Jude
1:3—12/24

REVELATION
 1:1—12/2
 1:7—12/5
 2:4—12/8
 4:3—12/11
 5:5—12/14
 6:2, 4–5—12/17
 6:7–8—12/20
 7:3—12/22
 11:3—12/27
 14:6—12/29
 15:3—12/30
 19:7—12/28
 22:3—12/31